D0323330

THE AGE OF FALLIBILITY

THE AGE OF FALLIBILITY

THE CONSEQUENCES OF THE WAR ON TERROR

GEORGE SOROS

Weidenfeld & Nicolson

LONDON

First published in the United States in 2006 by PublicAffairs

First published in Great Britain in 2006
by Weidenfeld & Nicolson

1 3 5 7 9 10 8 6 4 2

A CIP catalogue record for this book
is available from the British Library.

ISBN-13 978 0 297 85230 8
ISBN-10   0 297 85230 2

Printed in Great Britain by Mackays of
Chatham plc, Chatham, Kent

Weidenfeld & Nicolson

The Orion Publishing Group Ltd
Orion House
5 Upper Saint Martin's Lane
London, WC2H 9EA

www.orionbooks.co.uk

The Orion Publishing Group's policy is to use papers that are natural,
renewable and recyclable products and made from wood grown in sustainable
forests. The logging and manufacturing processes are expected to conform to
the environmental regulations of the country of origin.

Contents

Acknowledgments

I would not have been able to write this book without the help of my Personal Assistant, Yvonne Sheer. Michael Vachon has done a lot more than what you would expect from a Director of Communications. Other members of my staff including Douglas York, Dan Lustig, Wylia Sims, and Edward Sypniewski were also helpful in various ways.

I received valuable comments from a number of people whom I list in alphabetical order: Hakan Altinay, Zoe Baird, Kurt Biedenkopf , Emma Bonino, Robert Boorstin, Rosa Brooks, Maria Cattaui, Steven Clemons, Joan Dunlop, Yehuda Elkana, Sylvie Erb, Gareth Evans, Joseph Firestone, Roman Frydman, Misha Glenny, Karen Gordon, John Gray, Lani Guinier, Morton Halperin, Joost Hiltermann, Mary Kaldor, Anatole Kaletsky, Robert Kushen, Terje Larsen, Charles Leykum, Karin Lissakers, Mark Malloch Brown, Anthony Marx, William Maynes, Pierre Mirabaud, Kalman Mizsei, Ethan Nadelmann, Aryeh Neier, Howard Newman, Kalypso Nicolaidas, Wiktor Osiatynski, Christopher Patten, Istvan Rev, Anthony Richter, Jack Rosenthal, Thomas Scanlon, Laura Silber, John Simon, Robert Skidelsky, F. van Zyl Slabbert, Aleksander Smolar, Jonathan Soros, Mark Steitz, Herb Sturz, Strobe Talbott, Stuart Umpleby, Mabel van Oranje, Byron Wien, and Andre Wilkens.

I benefited from a discussion at the Central European University in Budapest with the following participants: Aziz Al-Azmeh, Sorin Antohi, Andri Chassambouli, Yehuda Elkana, Katalin Farkas, Eva Fodor, Janos Kis, Liviu Matei, Daniel Monterescu, Prem Kumar Rajaram, Howard Robinson, and Carsten Schneider; and an informal seminar in my home with Leon Botstein, Rosa Brooks, Troy Duster, Hendrik Hertzberg, Harold Koh, Gara LaMarche, Deborah Leff, Nicholas Lemann, Aryeh Neier, Peter Osnos, John Podesta, Simon Rosenberg, Mark Schmitt, Jennifer Soros, Jonathan Soros, and Michael Vachon.

PublicAffairs, and particularly its founder, Peter Osnos, excelled as usual.

April 2006
GEORGE SOROS

Prologue

Many people dream about making the world a better place, but I have been fortunate in being able to fulfill my dreams more than most. That said, my influence has been greatly exaggerated. I was labeled "the man who broke the Bank of England" when the United Kingdom was forced to leave the European Exchange Rate Mechanism. Mohamed Mahatir, the former prime minister of Malaysia, accused me of causing the Asian financial crisis of 1997. President Vladimir Putin of Russia holds me responsible for the so-called color revolutions in Georgia and Ukraine. And I was accused of trying to buy the election after I took a stand against the reelection of President George W. Bush in 2004. All these claims are overstated, or unfounded. For instance, I did not trade in Asian currencies for several months prior to the crisis so I could not have caused it. But the fact remains that I did play a role in some of these events, and many others. My foundations were active in the countries that formed part of the Soviet empire and supported the forces striving to turn those countries into open societies. They provided some cushion for culture, education, and science when the monolith of the communist state collapsed. They helped educate a new, self-conscious Roma (gypsy) elite. The Decade of Roma Inclusion, which brought together nine governments, the European Union and the World Bank in a concerted effort to improve the lot of the Roma, was my idea. During the Balkan wars of the nineties, my foundation, staffed by brave people, did what it could to ease the horror that befell Sarajevo. I have also been a moving force behind the Publish What You Pay campaign and the Extractive Industries Transparency Initiative. Rightly or wrongly, I have come to think that I can have an influence on the course of events, that I can have a policy.

How did I reach this privileged position? That is a long story and I have already told it in bits and pieces. To sum it up, I believe I combine three qualifications. First, I have developed a conceptual framework that has given me a certain understanding of history, and, in particular, what I call far-from-equilibrium situations; second, I have a set of firm ethical and political beliefs; and third, I have made a lot of money. Many people have one or two of these attributes, but the combination of all three is unusual. In addition, the network of nonprofit foundations I have established provides me with a firm base of local knowledge on the basis of which I can claim the right to be heard on a variety of issues. And the people who run these foundations have a right to participate in the political life of their country, a right that I, as an outsider, may not have.

In the early days, I was a loner. When the Soviet system collapsed, my foundations could accomplish a lot on their own; but when I tried to cooperate with other institutions or governments, I met with little success. Events moved too fast for people to keep up with them. For a long time my foundations were practically the only game in town, and that made them very influential; but when I proposed various policy initiatives, my suggestions usually fell on deaf ears. Since then, the situation has practically reversed. My ability to accomplish things on my own has greatly diminished, partly because I am taking on bigger issues and partly because I am not the only player on the field. On the other hand, I have acquired considerable convening power. I can help move issues forward by taking the initiative, or simply by participating. This allows me to form policy and take a stand on issues better than in the early days.

I should like to clarify where I stand. My goal is to make the world a better place. There is nothing unusual about that. Many people share my aspiration and work at it more selflessly than I do. What sets me apart is that I am able to do it on a larger scale than most others. When he was prime minister of Macedonia, Branko Crvenkovski, once described me as a stateless statesman. "States have interests but no principles," he said. "You have principles but no interests." I like that formulation and I try to live up to it. The world is badly in need of stateless statesmen.

Our society is suspicious of those who claim to be virtuous and not without justification. Many rich people who form foundations have ulterior motives for doing so. I like to believe I am different. Being able to do the right thing is a rare privilege, and exercising that privilege is ample reward. But I always tell people who question my motives that they are right to do so. When I claim to be disinterested, the burden of proof is on me.

As a stateless statesman, I face a number of obstacles. First, I am not really disinterested. I have to confess that I have a desire to make an impact and it gives me satisfaction to be involved in historical events. Second, I do not have perfect knowledge. I am bound to be wrong. I made my fortune in financial markets by understanding this and correcting my mistakes. In the area of world affairs, being wrong has more lasting consequences. Third, I recognize that no one has elected me or appointed me as a guardian of the public interest; I have taken on that role for myself. People are rightly suspicious of someone who can have a policy but is not accountable to the public. Nevertheless, I believe the common interests of humanity badly need looking after and it is better to do it imperfectly than not to try at all. One of my heroes, Sergei Kovalyov, once said to me, "All my life, I have been fighting for losing causes." He was a former Soviet dissident who then became ombudsman in the Russian Duma and played an important role in settling the first war in Chechnya. I try to follow in his footsteps. In the financial markets, I take positions in order to win. In the social sphere, I take positions because I believe in them whether I succeed or not. That is the difference between financial markets which are not governed by moral considerations and the social sphere where morality ought to play a role.

I am now over seventy-five years old and my personal time horizon is getting shorter. Therefore, I must draw a distinction between what I can hope to accomplish in my lifetime and the mission of my foundation network after I am no longer around. I am reluctant to define my own agenda because I should like to keep it open ended, but I must begin to define the agenda of my foundations because I will not be able to do it afterwards.

This book has helped me to clarify my agenda. Sometimes I see things clearly. At those moments I can take decisive action. This has happened many times in my financial career.

The best known example is when I "broke the Bank of England". It has also happened in my philanthropic and public life. The decisions to set up a network of open society foundations when the Soviet system collapsed and to oppose the re-election of President Bush stand out. When I sat down to write this book, I did not see things clearly; that is one of the reasons why I sat down to write it. By the time I finished I came to feel I am once again at such a moment. I realize what needs to be done and I am ready to do it, even if it means fighting losing battles. My hope and aspiration is that by the time the readers have fought their way through the book, they will come to feel the same way.

I have developed a philosophy that has played a central role in my life. It has guided me in making money and spending it, although it is not about money. I know how important that philosophy is for me personally, but I am still in the process of finding out whether it can have a similar significance for others. That is my first priority and this book is probably my final effort in this regard.

Translating my philosophy into a political agenda, I can define my goal as a global open society. I pursue it on two levels. One relates to the world order, the other to the order prevailing in individual countries.

I find the world order is frustrating as a practical agenda. It involves big ideas and many words, but they do not have much impact. My foundations are used to getting things done, and that is why I find talkfests debilitating. There is much more to be done in fostering open societies in individual countries. Conditions are not always favorable, but windows of opportunity open from time to time, and when that happens, I like to swing into action.

I must explain what I mean by a global open society. I emphatically do not mean a global government. Governments by their very nature interfere with individual freedom. When there are many countries to choose from, one can emigrate; but a global government would be oppressive almost by definition. I do mean the rule of international law. The prevailing world order is unsatisfactory. The neoconservatives (or neocons, as they are now called) are right on this point: International relations are governed by force, not by law. That has to change: international law must be enforced. That requires stronger international institutions than we currently have. Obviously we need the International Criminal Court (ICC); but we also need other institutions that are less obvious. The World Trade Organization (WTO) is a good example because it has an effective enforcement mechanism. The WTO is much criticized for being unfair to developing countries, and that needs to be remedied by changing the rules; but the structure itself is exemplary.

A global open society has to recognize that all rules are imperfect and subject to improvement. We also need rules for changing the rules, but they do not necessarily need to be codified because that could lead to an unending quibble about words. We already have a taste of it in the General Assembly of the United Nations. Let usage determine the rules—there is much to be said for common law in international relations.

I have described the frame for a global open society. It needs to be filled with content. Here I refuse to propose a timelessly valid prescription because every society and every generation has to define the meaning of open society for itself. The prevailing form of globalization is lopsided. Markets, especially financial markets, have become global, but the institutions that are needed for a society to flourish, or even to survive, have not. Political arrangements are based on the sovereignty of states; they are not sufficient to take care of the collective interests of humanity, such as peace, security, the environment, social justice, and even the stability of financial markets.

Sovereignty is an anachronistic concept; it has been inherited from an age when kings ruled over their subjects. In the French Revolution, the King was beheaded and the people took over the sovereignty of the state. Although it would be utopian to replace the people's sovereignty with something else, that principle, on its own, is inadequate for today's increasingly interdependent world. There are many concerns that transcend national borders. For instance, we are facing a global energy crisis. And within national borders, the rulers often abuse their power. When the abuse reaches the point where the people have no other recourse, the international community has a responsibility to intervene. This is a case for what Karl Popper has called piecemeal social engineering, and I am ready to engage in it personally and through my foundations.

I am always engaged in a large number of projects, and the list changes all the time. Some projects succeed, others fail. I tend to get more involved in those that make progress on their own and drop those that need too much pushing. For instance, I have supported the Community of Democracies ever since it was launched by the Warsaw Declaration in 2000 because I subscribe to its principles but as a project for the foundations, I always considered it marginal. After the 2005 conference in Chile, which was a useless talkfest, I was inclined to drop it, but after the formation of the United Nations Human Rights Council it may have a future after all. By contrast, the Publish What You Pay campaign launched in 2002 has developed into a successful movement against the misuse of revenues from natural resources and I have become deeply engaged in it.

Writing the book has helped me to establish future priorities. Some of them are quite far removed from our previous activities. I have identified two problems that endanger our survival: the global energy crisis and nuclear proliferation. As regards the former, we are already at the cutting edge of dealing with the resource curse and we are getting engaged in global warming. The Russian policy of using gas contracts both to suborn neighboring countries and to divert what ought to be public revenues for private benefit will be a particular field of interest. Nuclear proliferation, by contrast, has been entirely outside the purview of my foundations. I do not know what we can do about it but we cannot disregard it.

The main obstacle to a stable and just world order is the United States. This is a harsh – indeed, for me, painful — thing to say, but unfortunately I am convinced it is true. The United States continues to set the agenda for the world in spite of its loss of influence since 9/11, and the Bush administration is setting the wrong agenda. The Bush agenda is nationalistic: it emphasizes the use of force and ignores global problems whose solution requires international cooperation. The rest of the world dances to the tune the United States is playing, and if that continues too long we are in danger of destroying our civilization. Changing the attitude and policies of the United States remains my top priority.

The task has become more complicated since the 2004 elections, and that was the source of my confusion when I sat down to write this book. It is no longer a question of removing President Bush from the White House; a more profound rethinking of America's role in the world is needed. It is not enough to revert to the policies of the previous administration; America must undergo a change of heart. The process must begin with recognizing the war on terror as a false metaphor. It is now accepted that the invasion of Iraq was a grievous error but the war on terror remains the generally accepted policy.

The change of heart cannot be accomplished merely by helping the Democratic Party in the 2006 and 2008 elections because Democrats show no sign of engaging in a profound rethinking. On the contrary, Democrats have been so spooked by the Republican charge that they are soft on defense, that they are determined to outdo the Republicans in the war on terror. Nevertheless, I think it is important that the Democratic Party gain control of the House of Representatives in 2006. A Democratic-controlled House could reveal the misdeeds of the Bush administration which are currently kept under wraps.

Because of the way congressional districts have been gerrymandered, capturing the House will be no easy task in spite of the swing in public opinion against the Bush administration. Moreover, the Republican Party is supported by a well-financed conservative movement, and the Republic National Committee has an electoral machinery that is far superior to that of the Democratic National Committee. There is an urgent need to strengthen the Democratic Party in order to create a more level playing field. The financial restrictions imposed by the McCain-Feingold Act will make this difficult. The Republican National Committee will enjoy a continuing advantage because it built up its machinery before those restrictions went into effect.

The ultimate objective has to be to recapture the Republican Party from the conservative and religious extremists who now control it. American democracy is built on two parties competing for the middle ground. The system was undermined when extremists captured the Republican Party. If we are to restore the balance, the extremists must be routed. A resounding Democratic victory in 2006 would achieve that.

I do not feel comfortable about engaging in partisan politics, especially since the Democratic Party does not stand for the policies that I advocate; indeed, if it did, it could not be elected. I would prefer to be above politics. I feel obliged, however, to support the Democratic Party until the Republican Party is recaptured from the extremists. I should also like to support think tanks and advocacy organizations that could provide a counterweight to the conservative movement, but I do not want them to become a mirror image. If the conservative movement poses a threat to open society, a progressive movement that uses the same methods would merely reinforce the threat. Yet the conservative movement has proven itself very effective. How can a counterweight be equally effective yet abide by the principles of open society? That is a problem that baffles me.

My emphasis on the role of the United States as the source of stability in the world and the protector of our civilization is somewhat exaggerated on account of personal considerations. I chose the United States as my home, so I have a vested interest in justifying my choice. Moreover, I am obliged to adopt an American point of view when I am engaged in trying to influence American policy. But I am also a European. The failure of the United States to exercise the right kind of leadership has led me to believe that Europe could play a more important role, and if it did so, it could set an example that America could follow. The time may be right for launching a European open society foundation. I am also working on setting up an Arab Cultural Fund. A common language could bring closer together countries that are in danger of being torn apart by sectarian conflict, and culture could serve as a counterweight to the radicalization of Islam. Needless to say, both the European and Arab initiatives must have local sponsors and leaders. My foundation can provide only the initial impetus and funding.

The precipitous decline in the power and influence of the United States has made the world more unstable. I am a sponsor and supporter of the International Crisis Group (ICG), whose mission is to anticipate crises before they arise as well as to analyze them and suggest solutions. The landscape is crowded with incipient crises. I am particularly troubled by the increasingly authoritative and assertive direction Russia is taking. I wound down my foundation in Russia just in time to avoid persecution, but am committed to keeping the flame of freedom alive there. I am also ready to do what I can to help the countries of the "near abroad" that have been able to hold free elections to maintain their independence from Russia.

Originally, I did not want my foundations to survive me. I had grave reservations about philanthropy because it goes against the grain of the human character. We are selfish by nature, but philanthropists are supposed to act selflessly; this gives rise to all kinds of contradictions as well as a tendency toward hypocrisy. I felt that as a founder I was in a better position to protect the foundation against these pitfalls than a board guided by institutional responsibilities.

I have since changed my mind. I came to feel that I would be selfish if I allowed the foundation to die with me. After all, many people are devoting their lives to the foundation. Why should their work be terminated with my death? But that was not the deciding consideration, because I believe that the foundation staff should serve the mission of the foundation rather than the other way around. I realized that the foundations do have a mission which they could continue to fulfill without me. That mission is to support civil society in monitoring the performance of governments. That is an essential function of civil society in a democracy, but it is difficult to get support for it from other philanthropists, particularly in less-developed countries. I gained this insight in South Africa, where the ruling party has an absolute majority; nevertheless, the conditions of an open society are preserved by an independent judiciary and a civil society that is willing to hold the government accountable. Parallel to supporting civil society, the foundation should also assist governments in building their capacity. This is an initiative I hope to put in place during my lifetime.

Beyond these two activities, I hope the foundations will continue to engage in many others. Because I want the foundations to remain as entrepreneurial as they are now, I shall refrain from defining the scope of their activities in advance. Before I started writing this book, I did not know that I would hone in on the global energy crisis; how, then, can I predict what the foundation ought to focus on when I am not around?

Introduction

Since I recently celebrated my seventy-fifth birthday this is an appropriate time for reflection. I have had a full and interesting life. There is plenty to reminisce about, but my life is not yet over, and I am not ready to write my memoirs. In any event, I would not be very good at writing them. I have a singularly bad recall for past events. I like to joke that I remember only the future. My life has passed through many phases, and each one engaged me intensely at the time I lived it. Now that I am at yet another stage, I find it difficult to recreate the earlier ones, and I do not really want to. I still prefer to look forward rather than back.

I have an abstract turn of mind and concrete events matter to me only insofar as they provide some experience or insight that is relevant to my life. It is remarkable how many events I have lived through that have passed me by without leaving much of a trace. I have also made a point of not collecting documents that would help me refresh my memory or provide raw material for a biographer. I made that decision around 1984 when I set up a foundation in Hungary in support of a civil society against the Communist regime. People working in and around the foundation were taking considerable risks, and I felt that my foundation was about them, not about me. This attitude contributed to the success of the foundation. I now regret that I did not keep more of an archive because the foundation network has reached a size and importance that deserves to be properly documented. But it was the right decision at the time.

Instead of writing my memoir, I intend to expound and develop the conceptual framework that has guided me throughout my life. Since abstract ideas are difficult to communicate, I shall take an autobiographical approach. This has one major disadvantage. I shall not be able to avoid blowing my own horn; in autobiographical writing, there is nobody else to do it for me.

When I talk of expounding and developing my ideas, I have two distinct objectives in mind. Rightly or wrongly, I believe that I have gained some important insights, and I am eager to share them. At the same time, I am confronting issues that have no parallel in the past, and I feel the need to understand them better. This requires both a study of current problems and a revision and development of the framework I use. In the past, I have used my conceptual framework as a guide to action. Now that I have reached seventy-five, my scope for further action is limited. I should like this book to serve as a guide that not only I but also other people may use in their efforts to improve the world.

The problems that preoccupy me today include the war on terror, how to deal with the likes of Saddam Hussein, how to foster democratic development and alleviate poverty, and how to deal with global warming and nuclear proliferation. For some problems, I see possible solutions, other are deeply frustrating.

My biggest frustration is with the fundamental misconceptions that have prevailed in the United States in recent years. Misconceptions play a prominent role in my view of the world. I consider them causal factors in shaping the course of history. And I consider open society a desirable form of social organization exactly because of its ability to correct misconceptions. How is it that the oldest and most successful open society has become the victim of misconceptions?

In my last book, *The Bubble of American Supremacy*, I tried to pin the blame on the Bush administration. I called the war on terror and the invasion of Iraq temporary aberrations that would be corrected in the next elections. But President Bush was reelected. I must now dig deeper and explore what is wrong with contemporary American society. That is what I intend to do in this book.

My contention is that America has become a "feel-good" society unwilling to face unpleasant reality. That is why the public could be so grievously misled by the Bush administration. Unless this feel-good attitude can be changed, the United States is doomed to lose its dominant position in the world. There will be serious adverse consequences not only for America but also for the world.

To build my case, I must start at the deep end by exploring the relationship between thinking and reality. This will be an abstract, philosophical discussion, but if I am right in saying that misconceptions play a prominent role in history, I cannot avoid it. I contend that our understanding of reality is inherently imperfect and all human constructs are flawed in one way or another. Open societies recognize our fallibility, closed societies deny it. America is an open society, but people are not well versed in philosophy and they do not fully understand the principles of open society. That is how they came to be misled. To make that argument, I must explain the concept of open society.

I have made the philosophical discussion in Part One as readable as possible and it will help make the arguments in Part Two more powerful. For instance, I explain that the truth is not as self-evident as the Founding Fathers thought when they signed the Declaration of Independence. We have discovered since then that the truth can be manipulated. To persist in the pursuit of truth, we must realize that false metaphors and other misconceptions can have unintended adverse consequences. That awareness is lacking in a large part of the electorate. Those who are not interested in this argument should turn directly to the second part of the book.

In Part Two, I address what I consider to be the most pressing problems of the present moment in history: the present dangers to America as an open society; the failings of the European Union as an open society; the difficulties in spreading democracy; the lack of a legitimate international community capable of exercising the responsibility to protect; the global energy crisis, and nuclear proliferation. I cannot claim the same kind of validity for my views on these subjects as I do for the conceptual framework. It would invalidate my framework if I did. As a participant, I cannot avoid bringing my biases to bear. My bias is already visible in the selection of the problem areas.

Here is a broad outline of the main argument of Part Two: American has fallen into the hands of extremist ideologues, led by Vice President Dick Cheney and Secretary of Defense Donald Rumsfeld, who believe that the truth can be successfully manipulated. They have successfully manipulated a born-again president and a feel-good public. But there is a reality that exceeds their comprehension and that has rendered their policies counterproductive. The root cause of trouble is a false metaphor, the war on terror. It has done terrible damage to our standing in the world and endangered our open society at home; yet it is still generally accepted as the natural response to 9/11. I detail the damage and argue that it is largely self-inflicted by the willful misinterpretation of reality. We cannot start repairing the damage until we repudiate the false metaphor of the war on terror. We must do more than just revert to the policies we pursued prior to 9/11. We must recognize that as the dominant power in the world we have a special responsibility. In addition to protecting our national interests, we must take the leadership in protecting the common interests of humanity. I go into some detail as to what that entails.

Mankind's power over nature has increased cumulatively while its ability to govern itself has not kept pace. There is no other country that can take the place of the United States in the foreseeable future. If the United States fails to provide the right kind of leadership our civilization may destroy itself. That is the unpleasant reality that confronts us.

1

Conceptual Structures

PART I

Conceptual Framework

CHAPTER 1

Thinking and Reality

Our relationship to reality is more complicated than we realize. This holds true for humankind in general. American society in particular has developed some specific deficiencies in its attitude to reality. I propose to discuss the universal problem in the first part of the book and the specific problems of contemporary American society in the second part.

THINKING AS PART OF REALITY

By reality I mean everything that actually exists or happens. All conscious human beings, their thoughts and actions, are part of reality. This fact, that our thinking forms part of what we think about, has far reaching implications both for our thinking and for reality. It sets some insuperable obstacles to understanding reality and it also renders reality different from what we understand it to be. The latter distinction does not necessarily apply to all of reality. Some aspects of reality permit us to acquire knowledge but others are not amenable to dispassionate understanding, and reality as a whole belongs to that category. Exactly where the dividing line lies between what can and cannot be known is one of the things that cannot be known. Scientific method keeps making inroads into areas that were previously considered impenetrable. For instance, consciousness previously belonged to the realm of philosophy but now it has become the subject of scientific study.

Knowledge is represented by true statements. According to the correspondence theory of truth, statements are true if they correspond to the facts. To establish correspondence the facts and the statements which refer to them must be independent of each other. It is this requirement that cannot be fulfilled when our thinking is part of what we think about. This complication does not arise with regard to every aspect of reality. The movement of heavenly bodies and the hatching of eggs occur no matter what we think about them. They are the objects of knowledge.

The same cannot be said when we think about reality as a whole, or about phenomena that have human participants. When we ourselves participate in the events we think about, the complications become much more pervasive. Not only is our knowledge incomplete, but, more important, our imperfect understanding or fallibility becomes part of reality.

We cannot rely on knowledge alone when making our decisions. Reality is not independently given but is contingent upon our decisions. As a result, our decisions cannot correspond to what we would do if we possessed all the relevant facts. In other words, our behavior is not entirely rational. But this way of putting it is already a distortion of what human reason can accomplish. It assumes that decisions could, in principle, be based on a consideration of all the relevant facts. That is a distortion that is deeply engrained in the way we look at our relationship to reality. Indeed, the mere fact that we speak of a relationship between thinking and reality implies that our thinking is somehow separate from what we think about. That is not so. The relationship between thinking and reality is not between two separate entities but between a part and a whole. It is not reasonable to believe that we can acquire objective, dispassionate knowledge of something to which we belong, or that we can base our decisions on that knowledge. Yet this belief is widely held.

We have come to think of reality as something that is independent of our thinking in the sense that reality is out there waiting to be understood, and understanding reality consists of creating a picture in our mind that corresponds to it. This view is expressed in the correspondence theory of truth. Indeed, when thinking and reality are separate it is possible to formulate statements that correspond to the facts. For instance, consider this statement: "It is raining." It is a true statement. That works for some aspects of reality but not for others. When our thinking forms part of the reality we think about, the separation between thinking and reality is breached. Instead of a one-way correspondence between statements and facts there is a two-way connection. Now consider this statement, "You are my enemy." What I say may affect how you feel. The statement may correspond to a fact, but the correspondence does not signify knowledge because of the two-way connection. I may have turned you into an enemy instead of just passively recognizing that you are my enemy. The truth cannot be known because it is contingent on what we think. This puts the relationship between thinking and reality into a light very different from the one to which we have become accustomed. Our view of the world will never correspond to the world as it is because we are part of the world, and what we think automatically becomes part of what we have to think about. In trying to understand the relationship between thinking and reality, we are shooting at a moving target. The way we look at the world changes the world. This renders perfect knowledge unattainable. Nevertheless, it is possible to improve our understanding, even if we cannot attain perfection.*

THE CONCEPT OF REFLEXIVITY

Recognizing that our understanding of the world in which we live is inherently imperfect (fallible for short) constitutes a major step forward. Instead of thinking in terms of a one-way relationship in which our statements do or do not correspond to the facts, we need to take into account a connection that is going in the opposite direction. Our thinking makes an impact on the world in which we live. Not all aspects of reality are affected but those that are can be best understood in terms of a two-way relationship between thinking and reality.

On the one hand, we seek to understand our situation: I call this the cognitive function. On the other hand, we seek to make an impact on the world: I call this the participating

---

*Please note the difference in the way I use the words "knowledge" and "understanding." I do not want to define the difference—because it would get me into no end of trouble—so I will only indicate it. Knowledge is meant to be objective, understanding is admittedly subjective. Knowledge is connected with the correspondence theory of truth and scientific method; understanding is more personal and more biased. I say *more* biased because knowledge cannot avoid being biased either. Where knowledge is deficient, we have to fall back on understanding.

function. The two functions work in opposite directions, and they can interfere with each other. The cognitive function seeks to improve our understanding. The participating function seeks to make an impact on the world. If the two functions operated independently of each other, they could in theory serve their purposes perfectly well. If reality were independently given, our views could correspond to reality. And if our decisions were based on knowledge, the outcomes would correspond to our expectations. But that is not what happens because the two functions intersect: and where they intersect, they can interfere with each other. I have given the interference a name: reflexivity. The fact that I have given it a name does not mean that I have discovered something new; the phenomenon has been studied under different names since antiquity.

Reflexive situations are characterized by a *lack of correspondence* between the participants' views and the actual state of affairs. Take the stock market, for example. People buy and sell stocks in anticipation of future stock prices, but those prices are contingent on the investors' expectations. The expectations cannot qualify as knowledge. In the absence of knowledge, participants must introduce an element of judgment or bias into their decision-making. As a result, outcomes are liable to diverge from expectations. It is important to realize that reflexivity introduces an element of uncertainty and unpredictability not only into the participants' view of the world but also into the reality with which the participants contend. Reality can become far removed from what it would be if the participants based their decisions on knowledge alone.

Far-from-equilibrium Conditions

Mainstream economic theory is based on the assumption of rational behavior. That assumption allows economics to determine the equilibrium price. I contend that reflexive situations do not necessarily tend towards equilibrium; indeed, they can become far removed from what the theoretical equilibrium would be.* To describe such cases I speak of "far-from-equilibrium conditions." In financial markets, far-from-equilibrium conditions prevail often, but by no means all the time. I also apply the expression "far-from-equilibrium conditions" to political and social situations. Exactly when such conditions prevail is a fascinating question that has not been adequately studied because the concept of reflexivity has not been generally recognized.

I have devoted myself to the study of far-from-equilibrium conditions both in theory and in practice. I was exposed to them at an early age when Nazi Germany occupied Hungary in 1944, and I would have been exterminated for being a Jew if my father had not arranged for me to assume a false identity. What could be further from normal? Then I had a taste of the Soviet regime, with all its quirks and excesses, before I left Hungary and became a student at the London School of Economics. There, I was inspired by the philosophy of Karl Popper

---

*In the course of this discussion, I shall use the notion of equilibrium in various senses. Here I am referring to "rational expectations equilibrium" which assumes that apart from random deviations, market participants' expectations conform to an economist's model. Later I shall use it in the broader sense of perceptions corresponding to reality. Elsewhere I allude to a general equilibrium that assures the optimum allocation of resources. In all these senses equilibrium is unattainable. There is also the simple notion of an equilibrium price which clears the market; that equilibrium prevails in well-functioning markets all the time.

which, in turn, helped shape my own. When I became a hedge fund manager, I specialized in far-from-equilibrium situations in financial markets and made my fortune by understanding them better than most other market participants. As a philanthropist, I became involved in the collapse of the Soviet empire—a far-from-equilibrium process *par excellence*. In my book *Opening the Soviet System*, I drew an analogy with the boom-bust process that is characteristic of financial markets. More recently, I applied the same analogy in describing the Bush administration's policies after the terrorist attacks on September 11, 2001 (9/11 for short).

Reconsidering the Concept of Rational Behavior

Reflexivity occurs in a relatively narrow segment of reality, but it is the segment that has the greatest significance to us as participants. It is the situation in which we participate. That situation is characterized by an interference between the cognitive and the participating functions. As a consequence, our understanding of the situation is imperfect and our decisions have unintended consequences. The interference cannot be eliminated but by recognizing reflexivity we come closer to understanding reality than we do by postulating rational behavior.

If rational behavior is unattainable, how did it come to play such an important role in our view of the world? The answer is that rational behavior is an ideal condition that would eliminate unintended consequences. While perfect knowledge is beyond our reach, the more we know, the bet-

ter off we are. The pursuit of knowledge has been a distinguishing feature of our civilization.

Prevailing attitudes towards reality, knowledge and truth
have their roots in the Enlightenment. At the time of the Enlightenment, humankind had relatively little knowledge of or
control over the forces of nature, but scientific method held
out infinite promise because it was beginning to produce significant results. It was appropriate to think of reality as something out there waiting to be discovered. After all, not even
the earth had been fully explored in the eighteenth-century.
Gathering facts and establishing the relationship among
them was richly rewarding. Knowledge was being acquired
in so many different ways and from so many different directions that the possibilities seemed unlimited. Reason was
sweeping away centuries of superstitions and generating in
their place a triumphant sense of progress. The prevailing
view of the world set no limit to the cognitive function; it
recognized only a one-way connection between thinking and
reality and it treated reality as something independently
given that could be understood by making statements that
corresponded to the facts.

This point of view reached its apogee in logical positivism, a
philosophy that flourished at the beginning of the twentieth
century in Vienna. Logical positivism held that well-formed
statements were either true or false. Statements that could not
be put in either category were considered meaningless. Logical positivists treated facts and statements as different entities.
The only connection between the two was that true statements corresponded to the facts and false statements did not.

The possibility that statements also constituted facts was
largely, but not entirely, ignored. A lot of attention was paid

to the paradox of the liar. The paradox was first stated by Epimenides, the Cretan philosopher, when he said that Cretans always lie. If that was a fact, the statement was true. But if a Cretan philosopher could make a true statement, Cretans did not always lie; Epimenides' statement was therefore false. Bertrand Russell, the British philosopher who was responsible for bringing Ludwig Wittgenstein to Cambridge from Vienna offered a solution to the paradox of the liar. Russell drew a distinction between two classes of statements: self-referent statements and non-self-referent statements. Since the truth value of self-referent statements could not be unequivocally determined, he proposed that they should be excluded from the universe of meaningful statements. This solution might have served to preserve the pristine separation between facts and statements, but it would have prevented people from thinking about issues that concerned them, or even from being conscious of themselves. The absurdity of this position was highlighted by Ludwig Wittgenstein, who concluded his *Tractatus Logico-Philosophicus* by stating that those who understood the book had to realize that it was meaningless. Shortly thereafter, he abandoned logical positivism and became one of the founders of analytical philosophy.

The tradition of treating reality as something independently given remains deeply ingrained in our way of looking at the world. Take for instance, classical economic theory, which is built on the assumption of rational behavior. It started out with assuming perfect knowledge, an assumption that was seminal to nineteenth-century science.* Scientific

*Some important thinkers in twentieth century economics, however, recognized that knowledge is imperfect and that this leads to fundamental difficulties in defining economic rationality. For example, in his critique of socialist planning,

method, to be worthy of the name, was expected to produce unequivocal predictions and explanations. To determine the equilibrium price at which supply and demand are in balance, it was necessary to assume that people knew their own preferences and were fully cognizant of the opportunities that confronted them. It was taken for granted that the preferences and the opportunities were independent of each other. That was a reasonable position to take as long as all the preferences and opportunities were fully known. After all, they could not be fully known unless they were independently given.

It is now widely recognized that the assumption of perfect knowledge was unrealistic, but the idea that the scale of preferences and the range of opportunities are independent of each other has not been abandoned. Economists continue to search for the equilibrium point; when they cannot find it, they speak of multiple equilibria. I have tried to point out that there is a reflexive interconnection between values and opportunities, between the subjective and objective aspects of reality, as a result of which neither the prevailing values nor the available opportunities can be fully known and the equilibrium point cannot be determined. But my theory of reflexivity has not made much headway. Business schools teach it, but most academic economists ignore it.* This is not surpris-

---

Friedrich Hayek argued that there is a fundamental distinction between individual rationality and "the utilization of knowledge which is not given to anyone in totality." See *Individualism and Economic Order* (Chicago: University of Chicago Press, 1948). For related arguments, *see* Frank Knight, *Risk, Uncertainty and Profit* (Boston: Houghton Mifflin, 1921), and John Maynard Keynes, *The General Theory of Employment, Interest and Money* (New York: Harcourt, Brace, 1936).

*One exception is Roman Frydman. See Roman Frydman and Michael D. Goldberg, *Imperfect Knowledge Economics: Exchange Rates and Risk* (Princeton, NJ:

ing because the theory of reflexivity implies that the equilibrium price, especially in financial markets, cannot always be determined. Providing unequivocal predictions and explanations used to be the hallmark of scientific method, and academic economists are loath to abandon it. They are painfully aware that financial markets often trend away from a theoretical equilibrium rather than towards it, but they are reluctant to abandon the search for a theoretical equilibrium. Even their explanations of bubbles and other perturbations are couched in terms of equilibrium. Again this is understandable. Any discussion of dynamic disequilibrium implies a theoretical equilibrium. When I speak of far-from-equilibrium conditions, I am also invoking the concept of equilibrium. This shows how difficult it is to discuss reality without drawing a distinction between its objective and subjective aspects and without treating them as if they were independent of each other.

We have now lived through more than two hundred years

Princeton University Press, forthcoming 2007). The concept of reflexivity is better recognized in sociology. Alvin Gouldner, in his book published in 1970, *The Coming Crisis of Western Sociology* (New York: Basic Books), called for a *"reflexive sociology"*—which subsequently became an influential current in sociology in the 1970s and 1980s—because he recognized that sociologists are important actors in the social and political events they describe, and their engagement in the world changes the processes they study. Anthony Giddens argued that "social science is actively bound up with its subject matter, which in some part it helps reflexively to constitute". See *Modernity and Self-Identity: Self and Society in the Late Modern Age* (Stanford, CA: Stanford University Press, 1991). Harold Garfinkel, the most prominent representative of ethnomethodology, has contended that sociologists are like goldfish swimming in a bowl, confidently analyzing other goldfish, without having ever stopped to recognize the bowl and the water they have in common with the fish they study.

See also: *An Invitation to Reflexive Sociology* by Pierre Bourdieu and Loic Wacquant (Chicago: University of Chicago Press, 1992).

of the Enlightenment; during that time, the limitations of reason have become increasingly evident. Indeed, they were manifest almost from the beginning. The French Revolution renounced the old traditional arrangements and sought to impose a rational design on human affairs. The revolution started out with great enthusiasm, but it came to grief with the terror of 1794. There have been many grand designs since then, but none worked the way they were supposed to. It is time to recognize that our understanding of reality is inherently imperfect and that our decisions are bound to have unintended consequences. The Age of Reason ought to yield to the Age of Fallibility. That would be progress.

Unfortunately we have left the Age of Reason behind us without coming to terms with our fallibility. The values and achievements of the Enlightenment are being abandoned without something better being put in their place. In the social sciences and humanities, with the exception of economics, the attitude towards reality has swung to the opposite extreme. The post-modern idiom does not recognize reality, only narratives. I believe this view is just as false as the positivism of the Enlightenment. The truth lies somewhere in between. There is a reality, only it is beyond our reach. The extreme relativism of our post-modern society does not provide a satisfactory criterion for distinguishing between true and false, right and wrong. People are bereft and yearn for a greater degree of certainty. Today, America is led by a fearless leader who demands absolute trust and loyalty in the war on terror but the results of his policies are very different from what he has led people to expect. We have yet to understand the relationship between thinking and reality and learn to cope with our fallibility.

Fallibility

Fallibility has a negative sound. Indeed, every advance we make in better understanding the relationship between thinking and reality has a negative connotation because it involves a retreat from perfection. But this negative interpretation is itself a manifestation of our fallibility. Recognizing our fallibility has a positive aspect that ought to outweigh the loss of an illusory perfection. What is imperfect can be improved, and the improvement can manifest itself not only in our thinking but also in reality. If perfect understanding is beyond our reach, the room for improvement is infinite. My interpretation of reflexivity is basically optimistic—but I must admit that, as I grow older and make little headway with my interpretation, I am not immune to despair.

I have developed a coherent and self-consistent view of the world based on the twin principles of reflexivity and fallibility. It is neither perfect nor complete, yet it has carried me a long way in understanding reality and in participating in it. It has guided me both in the financial markets and in my philanthropy. I cannot judge to what extent my view of the world is original. After all, it deals with issues that everybody has to deal with. So much has been said on these subjects that it would be most unusual if anything I said turned out to be original. Indeed, what is original is bound to be idiosyncratic. Others must have said similar things in different ways. I have been influenced by many books. I acknowledge my indebtedness even though I have failed to list the references.

Nevertheless, I suspect that there may be something original in the way I have put the pieces together. I have come to this conclusion by observing that my conceptual framework is widely misunderstood. Many commentators say that I am merely embellishing the obvious. But that cannot be right because my framework is in conflict with some generally accepted theories, such as the theory that financial markets tend towards equilibrium; and my interpretation of specific situations, such as the war on terror, is at loggerheads with the prevailing wisdom.

KARL POPPER'S INFLUENCE

My thinking has evolved out of many influences and experiences. The most pervasive influence, other than my father's, came from Karl Popper, who was my tutor during my last year at the London School of Economics. Having lived through both Nazi and Soviet occupation in my native Hungary, Popper's book *The Open Society and Its Enemies* struck me with the force of revelation and prompted me to explore the author's philosophy. He argued that the Nazi and Communist ideologies have something in common—they both claim to be in possession of the ultimate truth. Since the ultimate truth is beyond human reach, both ideologies had to be based on a biased and distorted interpretation of reality; consequently, they could be imposed on society only by the use of repressive methods. He juxtaposed a different principle of social organization that is based on the recognition that claims to the ultimate truth cannot be validated. Popper called this principle "open society," and he held it out as preferable to a definitive design. He never defined exactly what an open society means; in view of our imperfect understanding, he did not like quibbling about definitions. In any case, an open society needs to be constantly redefined by the people who live in it, otherwise it might become a definitive design.

It is clear that the concept of an open society is closely associated with the concept of democracy, but it is an epistemological concept, not a political one. Historically, the concept of democracy has emerged out of a consideration for the role of power in society. People are liable to use their power to further their own interests, not the common interest. One way to protect the common interest is to insist on the division of powers. This became the cornerstone of the Constitution of the United States of America. Our Founding Fathers, particularly James Madison, John Adams and Thomas Jefferson, were acutely aware of our imperfect understanding, but that was not the foundation on which the Constitution was built. That is an important point to remember.

American democracy predates the concept of open society. The Constitution is a product of the Age of Reason; open society belongs to the Age of Fallibility. This difference has led to a curious result: America is an open society that does not fully understand the concept of open society; had America understood the concept, George W. Bush could never have enjoyed the kind of popularity he attained. As I shall argue, we have much to learn from the concept of open society.

The fact that open society is an epistemological concept is a source of both strengths and weaknesses. Its main strength is that it connects open society with the concepts of fallibility and reflexivity to provide a coherent view of the world without falling into the trap of a dogmatic ideology. Its main weakness is that it ignores the power relations that play such a crucial role in shaping events.

I have set up a network of foundations to promote the principles of open society, but our advocacy often runs up against the dictates of "realpolitik." I have come to realize that the principles of open society by themselves are inadequate as a guide to political action. In policy decisions, various considerations need to be weighed against each other; nevertheless, the principles of open society ought to be given greater weight than they have traditionally received.

Karl Popper was primarily a philosopher of science. I absorbed his ideas about scientific method as eagerly as I had responded to his idea of the open society, but I subjected his arguments to critical examination and parted company with him on a very important point. He proclaimed what he called the "doctrine of the unity of scientific method," namely, the same methods and criteria apply to the study of social affairs as to the study of natural phenomena. How could that be? The participants in social affairs act on the basis of imperfect understanding. Their fallibility introduces an element of uncertainty into social affairs that does not afflict the study of natural phenomena. The difference needs to be recognized.

I sought to express the difference by introducing the concept of reflexivity. The concept of self-reference had already been extensively analyzed. But self-reference pertains exclusively to the realm of statements. If the separation between the universe of statements and the universe of facts is a distortion of reality, then there has to be a similar effect in the realm of facts. That is the relationship that the concept of reflexivity seeks to express. Reflexivity is a feedback mechanism that affects not only statements (by rendering their truth value indeterminate), but also facts (by introducing an element of uncertainty into the course of events).

Reflexivity in Financial Markets

All this is highly abstract. Some illustrations are needed. In *The Alchemy of Finance*,* I cite many examples from the financial markets. Each case involves some type of short-circuit between the subjective and objective aspects of reality; usually, it manifests itself as a circular connection between the value attributed to entities and the entities themselves. They result in initially self-reinforcing, but eventually self-defeating, boom-bust processes.

One of my early successes as a hedge fund manager was in exploiting the so-called conglomerate boom that unfolded in the late 1960s. It started when the managers of some high-technology companies specializing in defense recognized that the historic growth rate their companies enjoyed could not be sustained in the aftermath of the Vietnam War. Companies such as Textron, LTV, and Teledyne started to acquire more mundane companies, and, as their per-share earnings growth accelerated, their price/earnings multiples, instead of contracting, expanded. They were the pathbreakers. The success of these companies attracted imitators; later on, even the most humdrum company could attain a high multiple simply by going on an acquisition spree. Eventually, a company could achieve a high multiple just by promising to put it to good use by making acquisitions.

Managements developed special accounting techniques that enhanced the impact of acquisitions. They also introduced changes in the acquired companies: They streamlined operations, disposed of assets, and generally focused on the

*My previous books, to which I often refer, are listed at the front of the book.

bottom line, but these changes were less significant than the impact on per-share earnings of the acquisitions themselves.

Investors responded like ducks to water. At first, the record of each company was judged on its own merit, but gradually conglomerates became recognized as a group. A new breed of investors emerged, the so-called go-go fund managers, or gunslingers, who developed a special affinity with the managers of conglomerates. Direct lines of communication developed between them and conglomerates placed "letter stock" directly with fund managers. Gradually, conglomerates learned to manage their stock prices as well as their earnings.

The misconception on which the conglomerate boom rested was the belief that companies should be valued according to the growth of their reported per-share earnings no matter how the growth was achieved. The misconception was exploited by managers who used their overvalued stock to buy companies on advantageous terms thereby inflating the value of their stock even further. Analytically, the misconception could not have arisen if investors had understood reflexivity and realized that inflated valuations can generate earnings growth.

Multiples expanded and eventually reality could not sustain expectations. More and more people became aware of the misconception on which the boom rested even as they continued to play the game. To maintain the momentum of earnings growth, acquisitions had to be larger and larger, and eventually conglomerates ran into the limits of size. The climactic event was the attempt by Saul Steinberg of the Reliance Group to acquire Chemical Bank: It was fought and defeated by the establishment.

When stock prices started to fall, the decline fed on itself.

The favorable impact of acquisitions on per-share earnings diminished and eventually it became impractical to make new acquisitions. The internal problems that had been swept under the carpet during the period of rapid external growth began to surface. Earnings reports revealed unpleasant surprises. Investors became disillusioned and managers went through their own crises: After the heady days of success, few were willing to buckle down to the drudgery of day-to-day management. As the president of one corporation told me: "I have no audience to play to." The situation was aggravated by a recession, and many of the high-flying conglomerates literally disintegrated. Investors were prepared to believe the worst, and for some the worst occurred. For others, reality turned out to be better than expectations, and eventually the situation stabilized. The surviving companies, often under new management, slowly worked themselves out from under the debris.

My best documented encounter with a boom-bust sequence is that of mortgage trusts. Mortgage trusts are a special corporate form brought into existence by legislation. Their key feature is that if they distribute 95 percent of the income they receive, they can distribute that income free of corporate taxation. The opportunity created by this legislation remained largely unexploited until 1969, when numerous mortgage trusts were founded. I was present at the creation and, fresh from my experience with conglomerates, I recognized their boom-bust potential. I published a research report, where I argued that the conventional method of security analysis tries to predict the future course of earnings and then to estimate the price that investors may be willing to pay for those earnings. This method is inappropriate to the analysis of mortgage trusts because the price that investors are willing to pay for the shares is an important factor in determining the future course of earnings. Instead of predicting future earnings and valuations separately, we shall try to predict the future course of the entire self-reinforcing process.

I then sketched out a scenario in four acts. It starts with an overvaluation of the early mortgage trusts that allows them to justify the overvaluation by issuing additional shares at inflated prices; then come the imitators, who destroy the opportunity. The scenario ends in widespread bankruptcies.

My report had an interesting history. It came at a time when go-go fund managers had suffered severe losses in the collapse of the conglomerates. Since they were entitled to a share in the profits but did not have to share in the losses of the funds they managed, they were inclined to grasp at anything that held out the prospect of quickly recouping their losses. They instinctively understood how a self-reinforcing process works because they had just participated in one and they were anxious to play. The report found a tremendous response, the extent of which I realized only when I received a telephone call from a bank in Cleveland asking for a fresh copy because theirs had gone through so many Xerox incarnations that it was no longer legible. There were only a few mortgage trusts in existence at the time, but the shares were so eagerly sought after that they nearly doubled in price in the space of a month or so. Demand generated supply, and a host of new issues came to market. When it became clear that the supply of new mortgage trusts was inexhaustible, prices fell almost as rapidly as they had risen. Obviously the readers of my report had failed to take into account the ease of entry, and their mistake was corrected in short order. Nevertheless, their initial enthusaism helped to get the self-reinforcing process described in the report under way. Subsequent events took the course outlined in the report. Mortgage trusts enjoyed a boom that was not as violent as the one that came after the publication of my report, but it turned out to be more enduring.

I had invested heavily in mortgage trusts and took some profits when the reception of my study exceeded my expectations. But I was sufficiently carried away by my own success to be caught holding a significant inventory of shares when the downdraft came. I hung on, and I even increased my positions. I continued to follow the industry closely for a year or so, and eventually sold my holdings realizing good profits. Then I lost touch with the group until a few years later when the problems began to surface. I was tempted to establish a short position, but I was handicapped because I was no longer familiar with the companies. Nevertheless, when I reread the report I had written several years earlier, I was persuaded by my own prediction; I decided to sell the group short more or less indiscriminately. Moreover, as the shares fell, I maintained the same level of exposure by selling additional shares short. My original prediction was fulfilled, and most mortgage trusts went broke. The result was that I reaped more than 100 percent profit on my short positions—a seeming impossibility since the maximum profit on a short position is 100 percent. (The explanation is that I kept on selling additional shares.)

A similar, circular connection between the act of valuation and the entities being valued could be observed in the great international bank lending boom and bust of the 1970s. Banks used so-called debt ratios to evaluate the creditworthiness of the borrowing countries, but they failed to realize that the debt ratios were affected by their own lending activities until it was too late. I analyzed the sequence of events and many other cases in *The Alchemy of Finance*, published in 1987. I have witnessed or participated in various boom-bust sequences since then, including the collapse of the European exchange rate mechanism in 1992, the emerging market crisis of 1997, and the Internet boom of the late 1990s, which turned into a bust in 2000.

A CONTEMPORARY EXAMPLE

I believe we are currently in the midst of a gigantic real estate bubble. It was caused by the determination of the Federal Reserve Bank not to allow a stock market decline in 2001 to turn into a self-reinforcing rout. The federal funds rate was lowered to 1 percent. Mortgage institutions encouraged mortgage holders to refinance their mortgages and withdraw the excess equity. They lowered their lending standards and introduced new products such as adjustable rate mortgages (ARMs), "interest only" mortgages, and promotional "teaser rates." All this encouraged speculation in residential housing units. House prices started to rise at double-digit rates. This served to reinforce speculation, and the rise in house prices made the owners feel rich; the result was a consumption boom that has sustained the economy in recent years. Again, the bubble can be attributed to a short-circuit between the value of assets and the act of valuation. This short-circuit is called the wealth effect.

REFLEXIVITY AS THE NORM

Reflexivity operates in real life as well, but it is more difficult to analyze and demonstrate than in the financial markets. The reason is that reflexivity is ubiquitous. It does not constitute a deviation from the norm; it is the norm. To appreciate this point, we must avoid the mistake of confusing reflexivity with the boom-bust process. Reflexivity comes in many shapes and sizes. In the financial markets there is a theory, equilibrium theory, which is falsified by the boom-bust sequences that occur from time to time. There is no similar theory to be falsified with regard to social conditions or historical events, although since the Enlightenment a general presumption of rationality has become deeply engrained in our view of the world and that presumption is challenged by the concept of reflexivity.

The Enlightenment saw reason as separate from reality. Although the brain is clearly part of the body, the mind was supposed to constitute a disembodied intellect capable of rational thought. That would not be possible without a cleavage between the mind and the brain. The way the brain works influences the way thoughts are expressed in language.

We do have the capacity to make statements that correspond to the facts. But that capacity is itself part of reality. We may pretend otherwise. We may claim that reason constitutes a disembodied intellect that is capable of attaining perfect knowledge, but that is a pretense that distorts reality.

Insights from Cognitive Science

We cannot form a picture of reality without distorting it. Recent discoveries in cognitive science have shown that the information we gather has to be processed before it can enter our consciousness. That is because information is received on a bandwidth of more than a million, but consciousness operates on a bandwidth of about forty. Experiments show that the processing takes about half a second; thus, our consciousness lags behind reality by that amount.* The lag is too large to allow consciousness to govern many of our reactions. Playing tennis or the violin requires behavior that is not controlled by consciousness; that is why tennis players and violinists have to practice so hard to develop their reflexes.

Consciousness is a relatively recent development in the animal brain. Far from being disembodied, the mind is deeply imbedded in more primitive brain functions. The connection between reason and the animal brain can be seen in the language we use in formulating our arguments. Up and forward are good, down and backwards are bad. Cognitive science discovered early that there can be no reason without emotion. In September 1848, Phineas Gage, the foreman of a construction gang building the Rutland–Burlington Railroad, set off an accidental explosion that blew his tamping iron through his head and destroyed most of his frontal lobe. Miraculously, his mental functions were not affected, but his personality changed and he became erratic and unreliable.† This case received a lot of

*Tor Norretranders, *The User Illusion: Cutting Consciousness Down to Size* (New York: Penguin, 1999).
†Antonio Damasio, *Descartes' Error: Emotion, Reason, and the Human Brain* (New York: Penguin Putnam, 1994).

attention. Since then, the connection between reason and emotion has been explored and exploited by the advertising industry and more recently by political operatives. Political operatives have discovered that it is more effective to appeal to the emotions than to reason. Framing the message has been developed into a fine art by Frank Luntz, who is a political consultant for right-wing organizations. He is responsible for catch phrases such as "tax relief," "death tax," the "Clear Skies Act," and "No Child Left Behind."

George Lakoff, a cognitive scientist, has exposed how Frank Luntz operates, but he has been less successful in coming up with antidotes. In their book, Lakoff and co-author Mark Johnson argue that the distinction between mind and brain is a fallacy that has led philosophy astray through the ages.* Fallacy it may be, but it has been a fertile one. The concept of the disembodied intellect opened an avenue to the pursuit of truth that has produced impressive results. Admittedly, a distortion of reality remained built into those results and we are still suffering from its consequences.

FERTILE FALLACIES

I call the separation of thinking and reality a fertile fallacy. It is not the only one. Fertile fallacies abound in history. I contend that all cultures are built on fertile fallacies. They are fertile because they flourish and produce positive results before their deficiencies are discovered; they are fallacies because our understanding of reality is inherently imperfect.

*George Lakoff and Mark Johnson, *Philosophy in the Flesh: The Embodied Mind and Its Challenge to Western Thought* (New York: Basic Books, 1999).

It follows from our fallibility that social arrangements cannot be based solely on knowledge or reason; they must also incorporate the accumulated biases of the participants. The collection of biases is commonly described as "culture." That is the basis on which I claim that all cultures are built on fertile fallacies.

Cultures differ. These differences serve as evidence that biases and other forms of imperfect understanding are important in shaping reality. But this observation alone does not prove anything. To supply the theory of reflexivity with content, something more is needed. I have tried to meet this requirement by analyzing far-from-equilibrium situations where perceptions are far removed from reality. Identifying such situations can go a long way to show that the prevailing interpretation of reality is somehow distorted. To this end, I have tried to apply my boom-bust theory to historical situations. In *Opening the Soviet System*, I analyzed the rise and fall of Soviet communism as a boom-bust process, and in *The Bubble of American Supremacy*, I compared the Bush administration's policies to a stock market bubble. These attempts may be insightful but they were less than conclusive because it is a distinguishing feature of the theory of reflexivity that it does not claim to yield determinate explanations or predictions.

EXPERIENCES OF FAR-FROM-EQUILIBRIUM SITUATIONS

I find my personal experiences more convincing. Far-from-equilibrium situations have played an important role in my life. Indeed, my experiences of far-from-equilibrium situations go back to before I was born. When the First World War broke out, my father, a very ambitious young man, volunteered to serve with the Austro-Hungarian army. He was captured by the Russians and taken as a prisoner of war to Siberia. Being ambitious, he became the editor of a newspaper produced by the prisoners. The paper was called *The Plank* because handwritten articles were posted on a plank; the authors hid behind the plank and listened to the comments made by the readers. My father became so popular that he was elected the prisoners' representative. When some soldiers escaped from a neighboring camp, their prisoners' representative was shot in retaliation. Instead of waiting for the same thing to happen in his camp, my father organized a group and led the breakout. His plan was to build a raft and sail down to the ocean, but his knowledge of geography was deficient; he did not know that all the rivers in Siberia flow into the Arctic Sea. They drifted for several weeks before they realized that they were heading to the Arctic, and it took them several months to make their way back to civilization across the taiga. In the meantime, the Russian Revolution broke out and they became caught up in it. Only after a variety of adventures did my father manage to find his way back to Hungary; had he remained in the camp, he would have arrived home much sooner.

My father came home a changed man. His experiences during the revolution affected him profoundly. He lost his ambition and wanted nothing more from life than to enjoy it. He imparted to his children values that were very different from those of the milieu in which we lived. He had no desire to amass wealth or to become socially prominent. On the contrary, he worked only as much as he needed to make ends meet. I remember being sent at Christmas time to his main client to borrow money for a vacation, and afterwards he was grumpy until he had earned enough to repay the loan. He spent a lot of time with his children. I used to join him after school at the swimming pool, and after swimming he would regale me with an installment of his Siberian adventures. He impressed on me that there are times when the normal rules do not apply, and if you obey the rules at those times you are liable to perish.

When Nazi Germany occupied Hungary in March 1944, my father put this precept to work. He was better prepared mentally than most others, and he did not hesitate to act on his beliefs. He obtained false identity papers and made arrangements for living with false identities, not only for his family but for many others. He charged some of his clients, but helped many others for no charge. I had never seen him busier. It was his finest hour.*

1944 became the formative experience of my life. I was fourteen and I had boundless admiration for my father. I absorbed and adopted his view of the world wholesale. As I have often said, the year of German occupation was a strangely positive experience for me. We were confronted by mortal danger and people perished all around us, but we managed not only to survive but to emerge victorious because we were able to help so many others. We were on the side of the angels and we triumphed against overwhelming odds. What more can a fourteen-year-old ask for?

*Tivadar Soros, *Masquerade: Dancing Around Death in Nazi-Occupied Hungary* (New York: Arcade Publishing, Inc., 2001). Originally published in Esperanto, *Maskerado Ĉirkaŭ la Morto: Nazimondo en Hungarujo* (J. Régulo, 1965 and Rotterdam: Universala Esperanto-Asocio, 2001).

After the heady adventures of the Nazi persecution, the situation began to deteriorate during the Soviet occupation. At first, the adventures continued, and we were able to maneuver successfully through perilous situations. The Swiss consulate employed my father to act as the liaison officer with the Russian occupying forces. The Swiss consulate was looking after the Allied interests at the time, so this was a key position. When the Allied Powers established their own representative offices, my father retired because he felt that if he worked for the Allies he would be too exposed. It was a wise decision—he avoided later persecution. But the situation was becoming drab and oppressive for a youth who had become accustomed to adventure. I also thought that it was unhealthy for a young man of fifteen to think exactly like his fifty-year-old father. I told my father that I wanted to get away. "Where would you like to go?" he asked. "To Moscow, to find out about communism, or to London because of the BBC," I replied. "I know the Soviet Union intimately and I can tell you all about it," my father said. That left London. It was not easy to get there but I arrived in September 1947.

Living in London was a comedown. I had no money and no friends. After my adventurous life, I was full of myself, but the people in London were not interested. I was an outsider looking in, and I discovered loneliness. There was a moment when I ran out of money. I was having a snack at a Lyons Corner House, and after paying for my food I had no money left. "I have touched bottom," I told myself, "and I am bound to rise. This will be a valuable experience." But it has turned out to be more of a hindrance than a help because from then on, I was anxious never to touch bottom again.

THE HUMAN UNCERTAINTY PRINCIPLE

I recount these events to show the experiences that have gone into shaping my conceptual framework. Nazi persecution, Soviet occupation, and being penniless in London all qualify as far-from-equilibrium situations. I learned at an early age that actual conditions can be very different from what can be normally expected, and the prevailing view is often inappropriate to actual conditions. The gap between perceptions and reality can sometimes become a chasm.

I became preoccupied with studying that gap. In developing the concept of reflexivity, I came to view fallacies and other misconceptions as a causal factor in shaping history. Indeed, I have come to overestimate the role of biased and distorted interpretations in determining events. I claimed that they gave history its unique, irreversible character; but this is undoubtedly a distorted view because many other factors are at work in history besides reflexivity. But it turned out to be a useful distortion because it drew my attention to a phenomenon that was strangely neglected at the time, namely, financial bubbles. My view of history qualifies as a fertile fallacy.

As we have seen, reflexivity introduces an element of indeterminacy or uncertainty into the participants' thinking and into the situation in which they participate. There is an uncertainty principle in operation in quantum physics as well, but that principle is different from the uncertainty principle in human affairs. Werner Heisenberg's uncertainty principle governs the behavior of quantum particles whether it is recognized or not. By contrast the behavior of thinking participants may be influenced by what they or others think about them. The human uncertainty principle poses an obstacle to the scientific study of human behavior. As I have already mentioned, I have been greatly influenced by Karl Popper and, on the whole, I accept his interpretation of scientific method more wholeheartedly than most contemporary philosophers of science, but I rue his failure to recognize the nature and significance of the obstacle.

REVISING POPPER'S SCHEME
OF SCIENTIFIC METHOD

Popper constructed a beautifully simple and elegant scheme of scientific method consisting of three elements and three operations. The three elements are the initial conditions, the final conditions, and the generalizations of universal validity, or scientific laws. The three operations are prediction, explanation, and testing. When the initial conditions are combined with scientific laws they provide a prediction. When the final conditions are combined with those laws they provide an explanation. In this sense, predictions and explanations are symmetrical. What is missing from this scheme is the verification of the laws. This was Karl Popper's special contribution to our understanding of scientific method. He asserted that scientific laws cannot be verified; they can only be falsified. That is where testing comes in. Scientific laws can be tested by pairing off initial conditions with final conditions. If they fail to conform to the scientific law in question that law has been falsified. One nonconforming instance may be sufficient to destroy the validity of the generalization, but no amount of conforming instances are sufficient to verify a generalization beyond any doubt. In this sense, there is an asymmetry between verification and falsification. The symmetry between prediction and explanation and the asymmetry between verification and falsification are the two salient features of Popper's scheme.

In my view, the contention that scientific laws cannot be verified counts as Popper's greatest contribution to philosophy. It resolves the otherwise insoluble problem of induction. Just because the sun has risen in the east every day since man can remember, how can we be sure that it will continue to do so? Popper's scheme removes the need for certainty. We can accept scientific generalizations as provisionally valid until and unless they have been falsified. This interpretation emphasizes the central role that testing plays in scientific method. It establishes a critical process that allows science to grow and to innovate.

Many features of Popper's scheme have been criticized by professional philosophers. For instance, Popper maintains that the more severe the testing a generalization survives, the greater its value. Professional philosophers question whether the severity of tests and the value of generalizations can be measured. Nevertheless, Popper's assertion makes perfect sense to me and I have proved it in the financial markets. The more the investment hypotheses I adopted were in conflict with the generally prevailing view, the greater the financial rewards I earned when the hypotheses proved to be correct. It is on these grounds that I can claim that I accept Popper's scheme more wholeheartedly than the professional philosophers.

As noted, I part company with Popper only on one point. He asserts what he calls the doctrine of the unity of method, that is, the same methods and criteria apply to the social sciences as they do to the natural sciences. I beg to differ. I believe that what I have called the human uncertainty principle introduces an obstacle that is unique to the social sciences; it drives a wedge between the natural and social sciences. Exactly where the wedge is located is in dispute. On which side do the life sciences, such as genetics, fall? There need not be a firm dividing line to claim that the social sciences face an obstacle, the human uncertainty principle, that is absent in the natural sciences.

But scientific method is not the main issue. How can participants make the best decisions when they cannot base their decisions on knowledge? That is the crux of the matter. A gap between perception and reality is inevitable, and it is bound to cause some discrepancy between outcomes and expectations. It is the size of the gap and the severity of the unintended adverse consequences that matters. How can they be kept to a minimum? That is the question that has preoccupied me in theory and in practice.

It is in this context that I have found Popper's scheme of scientific method so inspiring. He demonstrates that even in natural science, where it is possible to establish a correspondence between statements and facts, it is essential to preserve a critical process and a critical attitude. How much more important is it to engage in critical thinking in other spheres where the uncertainties are much greater? This leads me to the concept of open society, which is based on the recognition that nobody is in possession of the ultimate truth.

THE POSTULATE
OF RADICAL FALLIBILITY

I shall elaborate the concept of open society in the next chapter, but before I do so I want to make one additional point about imperfect understanding, or fallibility. On the whole I agree with Popper's position, but I take it one step further. He asserts that we *may* be wrong. I adopt as my working hypothesis that we are *bound* to be wrong. I call this the postulate of radical fallibility. I base it on the following argument: We are capable of acquiring some insight into reality, but the more we understand, the more there is to be understood. Confronted by this moving target, we are liable to overburden whatever knowledge we have acquired by extending it to areas where it is no longer applicable. In this way, even valid interpretations of reality are bound to give rise to distorted ones. This argument is similar to the Peter Principle, which holds that competent employees are promoted until they reach their level of incompetence.

I find my position buttressed by the findings of cognitive linguistics. George Lakoff, among others, has shown that language employs metaphors rather than strict logic. Metaphors work by transferring observations or attributes from one set of circumstances to another and it is almost inevitable that the process will be carried too far. This can be best seen in the case of scientific method. Science is a highly successful method for acquiring knowledge. As such, it seems to contradict the postulate of radical fallibility, namely that we are bound to be wrong. But the process has been carried too far. Because of the success of natural science, social scientists have gone to great lengths to imitate natural science.

Consider classical economic theory. In its use of the concept of equilibrium, it is imitating Newtonian physics. But in financial markets, where expectations play an important role, the contention that markets tend towards equilibrium does not correspond to reality. Rational expectations theory has gone through great contortions to create an artificial world in which equilibrium prevails, but in that world reality is fitted to the theory rather than the other way round. This is a case to which the postulate of radical fallibility applies.

Even when they failed to meet the rules and standards of scientific method, social thinkers sought to cloak their theories in scientific guise to gain acceptance. Sigmund Freud and Karl Marx both asserted that their theories determined the course of events in their respective fields because they were scientific. (At that time, scientific laws were expected to be deterministic.) Popper was successful in unmasking them, particularly Marx, by showing that their theories could not be tested in accordance with his scheme; therefore they were not scientific. But Popper did not go far enough. He did not acknowledge that the study of social phenomena encounters an obstacle that is absent in the natural sciences—the human uncertainty principle. As a consequence, the slavish imitation of natural science does not produce an adequate representation of reality. General equilibrium and rational expectations are far removed from reality. They provide examples of how an approach that produces valid results becomes overexploited and overburdened to the point where it is no longer valid.

Suppose my objections to the concepts of general equilibrium and rational expectations were generally upheld and the theories were abandoned; they would no longer serve as examples of radical fallibility. This shows the fatal flaw in my postulate: It is not necessarily true. Just as Popper did not go far enough, I went too far. We are not bound to be wrong in every situation. Misconceptions can be corrected.

Where does that leave my postulate? If it were a scientific theory it would be proven false because in Popper's scheme a single instance is sufficient to falsify a theory. But the postulate of radical fallibility is not a scientific theory. It is a working hypothesis and, as such, it works remarkably well. It emphasizes the divergence between reality and the participants' perception of reality and it focuses attention on misconceptions as a causal factor in history. This leads to a particular interpretation of history that can be illuminating. The present moment is such a time. I regard the war on terror as a misconception, or false metaphor, that is having a nefarious effect on America and the world.

The radical fallibility idea is equally useful in financial markets. It points to the role of misconceptions in boom-bust processes. It directs us to look for the flaw in every construct, be it a theory or an institution; yet it should not discourage us from trying to improve them. And it should protect us from considering any proposition or arrangement as timelessly valid. We need a conceptual framework that claims to be timelessly valid if we are to make sense of an otherwise confusing universe, but we must recognize that it is bound to be distorted and incomplete and therefore in need of revision. My framework meets these requirements. If the postulate of radical fallibility were a scientific theory, it would provide its own falsification like the paradox of the liar.

The postulate of radical fallibility and the idea of fertile fallacies are peculiar to my way of thinking. These concepts sound negative, but they are not. What is imperfect can be improved; radical fallibility leaves infinite room for improvement. In my definition, an open society is an imperfect society that holds itself open to improvement. Open society engenders hope and creativity, although open society is constantly endangered, and history is full of disappointments. In spite of the negative-sounding terminology—imperfect understanding, radical fallibility, fertile fallacies—my outlook on life is profoundly optimistic. That is because from time to time I am able to bring about improvements in real life.

The Pursuit of Truth

The question remains: What is the significance of my conceptual framework? I can testify to its personal significance. The pursuit of truth through a critical process is a deeply held conviction that has guided me throughout life. So is the insight that the ultimate truth is unattainable. As part of the critical process, I have asked myself why is it so important to pursue the truth. The question is a valid one. In scientific method, the truth matters above all: A scientific theory is valuable only if it is valid. Not so in politics and other aspects of social life. False ideas can prevail. What is more important: to pursue the truth or to prevail? The answer is not obvious. Each person and each society has to establish its own priorities. I have no doubt where my own priorities lie. As a matter of personal choice, I have a deep commitment to the truth. I do not necessarily have to speak it, but at least I want to know it. The man I admire most is Andrei Sakharov, the Russian nuclear scientist, who insisted on speaking the truth even if it hurt him; I should like to imitate him but I do not have his strength of character. Speaking the truth can be hurtful not only to oneself but also to others, so discretion may be the better part of valor. Nevertheless, I have made a point of speaking out on political issues, notably in opposition to President George W. Bush. I have done so because I felt I was in a better position than most of the others who could have made themselves heard. I was not dependent on government or business contacts. I could afford to take the heat.

What I cannot judge is whether my conceptual framework holds any interest for others. The extent to which my interpretations of reality have been at odds with the generally prevailing ones, particularly with regards to the war on terror, but also in the financial markets, makes me think that I must be saying something significant and perhaps even original. I am aware, however, that in examining the relationship between thinking and reality I am covering well-trodden ground. Some of the issues I explore have been discussed at great length. The concept of self-reference has preoccupied philosophers since ancient times. Similarly, speech acts (namely that speech constitutes action) have been widely recognized. Nevertheless I believe that the two-way feedback mechanism I call reflexivity has not received the attention it deserves.

The Problem of Death

To test whether my conceptual framework can carry the same kind of meaning for others as it does for me I should like to submit my views on death for my readers' consideration. Mortality is an important issue when one is seventy-five, but it became an issue for me at a much earlier age, when I first discovered that my parents were mortal. As a child, I trusted them, relied on them, and tried to please them, but what right had they to bring me into this world if they intended to die and leave me alone in it? I felt betrayed. Since religion was not part of our family life (my mother became religious later), the prospect of death cast a deep shadow on my existence. It separated my adolescence from my childhood. I had been a happy, outgoing child, secure in my parents' love. My adolescence was more troubled. I could practically feel the ends of my lips turning down from a smile into a grim and somber expression. I engaged in a profound contemplation of life and death, as adolescents often do. The problem of death has weighed upon me ever since, although when I developed my conceptual framework I found an intellectually satisfying solution for my mortality.

Here it is. The idea of death is simply unacceptable to human consciousness because it is the annihilation of that consciousness. Death renders all our ideas, including our idea of reality and self, nonexistent. It is anathema, something that cannot even be contemplated. But the discovery that there is an inherent divergence between our views of the world and the world as it is casts the problem in a new light. The idea of death is not the same as the fact of death. The idea of death is the denial of consciousness, and the fact of death is not the denial of life but its natural conclusion. If death comes at a time when all passions are spent, it need not be terrifying. Although I found this interpretation of death intellectually satisfying, the prospect of dying continues to weigh on me because my passions are not yet spent. I wonder whether other people find this view as intellectually satisfying as I do.

CHAPTER 2

The Meaning of Open Society

The meaning of open society is obvious to those who have lived in a closed society. Open society denotes freedom and the absence of repression. When I set up a network of foundations in the former Soviet empire, I did not think it necessary to explain the concept of open society to the people concerned because it was the opposite of everything they had experienced. When repression ceases, the memory of it fades as time goes on. The United States is an open society, but people have little understanding of the concept, and even less commitment to it.

Open society is not an easy idea. It resembles the concept of liberal democracy but there is an important difference: it is an epistemological concept, not a political one. It is based on the recognition of our imperfect understanding, not on a political theory. This poses considerable philosophical and practical difficulties. The best way to explicate them is to provide a historical account.

As already mentioned, I was introduced to the concept of open society by Karl Popper. His book, *The Open Society and Its Enemies*, made a deep impression on me because it threw a new light on the ideologies that had had such a decisive influence on my life: fascism, national socialism, and communism. He argued that these ideologies shared a common feature: They asserted that they were in possession of the only valid interpretation of reality, and they demanded absolute loyalty to their point of view. But the ultimate truth is beyond human reach; therefore these ideologies could be imposed on society only by the use of force or other forms of compulsion. And repression serves to bring about a closed society.

Popper proposed a form of social organization that starts with the recognition that no claim to the ultimate truth can be validated and therefore no group should be allowed to impose its views on all the rest. He called this form of social organization the open society in which people of different views and interests are able to live together in peace. In an open society, individuals enjoy the greatest degree of freedom that is compatible with the freedom of others. What constraints are needed are set by the rule of law.

The term "open society" was first used by Henri Bergson, the French philosopher, in his book *Two Sources of Morality and Religion*, published in 1932. He argued that morality and religion could be based either on tribal identity or on considerations of the universal human condition. The Old Testament was an example of the former, the New Testament of the latter. Tribal morality gave rise to a closed society, which confers rights and obligations on members of the tribe and discriminates against outsiders; universal morality leads to an open society that recognizes certain fundamental human rights regardless of tribal, ethnic, or religious affiliations. Popper took the argument a step further: He made the point that universal ideologies such as communism could also pose a threat to open society if they claimed to represent the incontrovertible truth and if they discriminated against those who disagreed with that claim. He based the argument for open society on our inherently imperfect understanding, or fallibility.

Karl Popper did not give a definition of open society because he disliked definitions. It follows from our fallibility that any definition is bound to be distorted or incomplete and it is liable to give rise to an interminable debate about the meaning of words. Popper preferred to describe ideas, and then he liked to put a label on them. His method went from right to left, instead of from left to right. When he described various intellectual positions, he used labels, and they usually ended with an "ism"; indeed, Popper's writings are loaded with "isms." As a label, "open society" gained added significance because it found its way into the title of Popper's book. Apparently, *The Open Society and Its Enemies* was not the only title Popper contemplated, but the choice was made by the publisher. So open society attained the significance it holds for me almost by accident. I found it alluring because it stood in contrast to fascism and communism, and I had suffered under both. It may be fair to say that I put greater weight on the concept of open society than Karl Popper himself did.

In Karl Popper's writings, open society is not a fully developed concept. It is based on the idea that perfect knowledge is beyond the reach of the human intellect. An open society accepts our fallibility; a closed society denies it. It is not even clear whether open society is meant to denote an actual state of affairs or an ideal one. It cannot be a full representation of reality because it is based on only one aspect of reality, an abstract and philosophical aspect, and leaves other aspects, such as political power or historical context, out of account.

I have to confess that it took me a long time to recognize that the concept of open society lacks a proper grounding in political theory. It is only recently that the full implications of this fact dawned on me. When I first read *The Open Society and Its Enemies*, I was so impressed by it that I elaborated a conceptual framework juxtaposing open society and closed society. I will summarize the framework here. Readers who are interested in a fuller version can turn to the appendix.

The framework was built on the concept of change. I defined change to exclude everything that is predictable. This means that only events that could not be expected in accordance with the prevailing state of knowledge qualify as change.

First, I considered a society built on the absence of change. In such a society, the mind has to deal with one set of conditions only: that which exists at the present time. What has gone before and what will come in the future are perceived as if they were identical to what exists now. There is no need to distinguish between thinking and reality; there is no room for abstract thinking. What I called the traditional mode of thinking has only one task: to accept things as they are. This supreme simplicity extracts a heavy price: It generates beliefs that may be completely divorced from reality. The traditional mode of thinking can prevail only if members of a society identify themselves as part of the society to which they belong and unquestioningly accept their place in it. I called this an "organic society," a society in which individuals are organs of a social body.

Whether organic societies ever existed in reality or only in our imagination is an open question. But if they existed at all, they were certainly vulnerable to forms of social organization that had a better grasp of reality. So however attractive some features of an organic society may be to some people, organic society is not an option for today.

Change, the way I defined it, breeds uncertainty. There are two ways to deal with uncertainty: We can accept it or deny it. The former leads to a critical mode of thinking and to an open society; the latter to a dogmatic mode and a closed society. Each approach has its merits and drawbacks. Inspired by Karl Popper, I constructed a framework of theoretical models that contrast the strengths and weaknesses of the two approaches.

In a changing world, people are confronted by an infinite range of possibilities. Choosing among them is the key function of the critical mode of thinking. The great merit of the critical process is that it can provide a better understanding of reality than the traditional or the dogmatic mode. Its major drawback is that it does not satisfy the quest for certainty. In my model, I examine how the critical process works in some of the major fields of human endeavor, notably natural science, social science, economics, and politics. It works best in natural science, but it does not live up to expectations in the other areas. This is a source of disappointment that drives people to a dogmatic mode of thinking. The dogmatic mode is in many ways the opposite of the critical mode: It gives people the illusion of certainty but it distorts reality.

An open society recognizes and accepts the uncertainty inherent in reality. It is characterized by institutions that allow people to cope with uncertainty. Economic activity is guided by markets in which participants are free to make their own decisions. As long as there are enough choices available, participants can allocate their resources to their best advantage. Financial markets provide an efficient feedback mechanism for deciding whether or not their investment decisions were correct. But markets are not perfect. Contrary to some economic theories, they do not assure the optimum allocations of resources. They are designed to offer the participants alternatives, but the participants do not enjoy perfect knowledge. This makes markets, particularly financial markets, inherently unstable. Moreover, markets are not designed to take care of social needs—such as the maintenance of law and order, the protection of the environment, social justice, and stable and competitive markets—as distinct from the needs of individual participants. The satisfaction of social needs is in the domain of politics.

The political system appropriate to an open society is a democracy in which people are free to choose—and to change—their government. A democratic form of government is more likely than other forms to avoid grievous mistakes.

Thus, the main merits of an open society are that it allows people to cope with an uncertain reality and assures them the greatest possible degree of individual freedom compatible with the satisfaction of social needs. In particular, an open society insists on the freedom of thought and expression.

On the negative side, the paramount position enjoyed by individuals imposes a burden on them that may at times appear unbearable. Where can they find the values they need to make the correct choices? Values are a matter of choice. The choice may be conscious and the result of much soul-searching and reflection; but it is more likely to be impulsive, based on family background, advice, advertising, or some other external influence.

Recent findings in cognitive science indicate that the way decision-making works has some similarities with vision. Just as there is central vision which is sharp and enters into a central consciousness; peripheral vision is blurred and perceived selectively. In the same way, some decisions are conscious, others are instinctive. We know the reasons for our conscious decisions, but we make many choices of which we are only dimly aware. Marketing experts and political operatives focus on the unfocussed. Some of these choices are driven by the search for pleasure. But when we go beyond choices that provide immediate satisfaction, we find that open society suffers from what may be termed a deficiency of purpose. By this I do not mean that no purpose can be found, but merely that it has to be sought and found by each individual. This search places us in a quandary. Individuals are the weakest units of a society and have shorter life spans than most of the institutions that depend on them. On their own, individuals provide an uncertain foundation for values sufficient to sustain a structure that will outlast them. Yet such a value system is needed to sustain society.

Whether an open society can flourish despite its deficiency of purpose depends greatly on its ability to generate a pervasive sense of progress. Freedom releases creative energies, and open societies are usually characterized by scientific and artistic achievements, technological innovations, intellectual stimulation, and improved living standards. But success is not assured because it remains conditional on the creative energies of the participants.

When an open society fails to produce a sense of well-being and progress, those who are unable to find a purpose in themselves may be driven to a dogma that provides them with a ready-made set of values and a secure place in the universe. The dogmatic mode of thinking consists of establishing as paramount a body of doctrine that is believed to originate from a source other than the individual. The source may be tradition, or it may be an ideology that succeeds in gaining supremacy in competition with other ideologies. Either way, the source is declared the supreme arbiter of conflicting views: Those that conform are accepted; those that are in conflict, rejected. If an ideology manages to prevail, it can remove the fearful specters of uncertainty and deficiency of purpose and infuse people with a sense of pride and satisfaction. On the negative side, closed societies tend to exercise close control over speech and thought and engage in various forms of repression in order to impose their version of the collective interest over the interests of individual citizens.

No matter how the collective interest is defined in theory, in practice it is likely to reflect the priorities of the rulers. The rulers are not necessarily furthering their selfish ends as individuals, but they do benefit from the prevailing system as a class: By definition, they are the class that rules. Closed society may therefore be described as a society based on class exploitation.

At its best, an authoritarian system can go a long way towards reestablishing the harmony of organic society. But more often some degree of coercion must be employed, and this fact needs to be explained away by tortuous arguments that render the ideology less convincing. The result is that more force is applied until, at its worst, the system is based on compulsion and its ideology bears no resemblance to reality.

As the coercion employed to maintain the dogma increases, the needs of the inquiring mind are less likely to be met. When finally the hegemony of a dogma is broken, people will feel that they have been liberated from terrible oppression. Wide new vistas are opened and the abundance of opportunities engenders hope, enthusiasm, and tremendous intellectual activity.

The open society and the closed society present themselves as alternatives. Each suffers from deficiencies that can be cured by the other. This was appropriate at the time I constructed the models because the camps representing the two forms of social organization confronted each other in the Cold War, but it is not necessarily true at all times. If we build models of society based on a dichotomy between recognizing or denying that our understanding of reality is inherently imperfect, then the models are bound to appear as alternatives. It does not follow that people are obliged to use such models for their thinking.

Unfortunately, it is not clear what the framework (discussed in greater detail in the appendix) is supposed to represent. It cannot claim to describe historical situations. I made no attempt to provide evidence that any of the models have ever existed in their pure form, and I expressly disclaimed that the models could be used to describe a pattern in history. These were meant to be theoretical models, derived from the idea of fallibility largely by the use of deductive logic, yet they did not totally lack a historical perspective. Notably, organic society and a traditional mode of thinking had to precede closed society and a dogmatic mode of thinking. The whole framework had a particular relevance to the moment in history when it was constructed. During the Cold War, two competing social systems, based on two different modes of thinking, were competing against each other. Conceived when communism was at the height of its influence, the framework is balanced in its presentation of the strengths and weaknesses of open and closed societies. I made no secret of my bias in favor of open society, but I did not predict its inevitable triumph (that is just as well, since open society is once again endangered). In spite of its shortcomings, this was the conceptual framework that guided me when I established the Open Society Foundation.

The Follow Up

The conceptual framework outlined here and presented at greater length in the appendix formed part of a manuscript titled *The Burden of Consciousness*, which I completed in 1963. I sent the manuscript from New York, where I was working as a specialist in foreign stocks, to my erstwhile tutor, Karl Popper. I received an enthusiastic acknowledgement, which prompted me to visit him in London. At the appointed time, several graduate students were waiting for him, and they looked at me as an unwelcome intruder. I went into the corridor, and when Popper stepped out of the elevator, I introduced myself. It was obvious that he did not remember me. When he connected me to the manuscript I had sent him, he said: "I am so disappointed, and I shall explain to you why—I thought you were an American, to whom I had successfully communicated my views on totalitarian dictatorships. But you are Hungarian, and you experienced them at first hand." Nevertheless, he was very kind and encouraging.

Responding to his encouragement, I continued to revise the manuscript, but I could never resolve the basic ambiguity inherent in the models: Are they timelessly valid generalizations or are they idealized versions of historical situations? I got lost in philosophical abstractions. I decided to quit and devote myself to making money. This led me to develop the boom-bust model that eventually formed the subject of my first book, *The Alchemy of Finance*.

My success in the financial markets exceeded my expectations. As I was approaching fifty and the size of my hedge fund was approaching $100 million, I started wondering what I should do with the money I was earning. My personal wealth was around $30 million at the time, and I felt that it was more than sufficient for me and my family. I thought long and hard about what I really cared about. This took me back to the framework of open and closed societies; I set up an Open Society Fund and defined its objectives as follows: to open up closed societies; to make open societies more viable; and to promote a critical mode of thinking.

THE OPEN SOCIETY FOUNDATION

The Open Society Foundation got off to a slow start. My first major engagement was in South Africa, where, after an exploratory visit in 1979, I gave scholarships to African students attending the University of Cape Town. South Africa was a closed society in which whites lived in the first world and blacks in the third. I wanted to break down the barrier by giving Africans a first-class education and I tried to use the system to undermine it from the inside. All students, whether white or black, were entitled to free university tuition. I wanted to take advantage of this provision by giving African students stipends so that they could attend Cape Town University—an institution that proclaimed its commitment to the ideal of an open society. Unfortunately, the black students remained alienated and resentful, and when I found that out, I abandoned the scheme. I came to the conclusion that the apartheid regime was too strongly entrenched to be subverted from the inside. After the collapse of the apartheid regime, I regretted that decision.

I continued a few other initiatives in South Africa, but concurrently with them, I started supporting dissidents in Eastern Europe, including Charta 77 in Czechoslovakia, Solidarity in Poland, and Jewish Refuseniks in the Soviet Union. I became active in Helsinki Watch, the precursor of Human Rights Watch. I offered scholarships in the United States to dissident intellectuals from Eastern Europe, and this was the program that led me to establish a foundation in my native country, Hungary, in 1984. The scholarship scheme supplied me with a group of trusted advisers on whom I could rely in my negotiations with the Communist authorities in Hungary. The negotiations were protracted and they resulted in a complicated arrangement with the Hungarian Academy of Sciences as my partner. We established a joint committee, an official of the academy and myself as co-chairmen. The rest of the board members were independent-minded Hungarian intellectuals, approved by both parties. Both parties had the right of veto over the decisions of the committee. The question of who would execute the decisions was a thorny one, and it nearly caused a breakdown in negotiations. Eventually, we were allowed to have an independent secretariat; but since the academy also had to be represented on it, the academy's representative, as well as our secretary, had to sign communications.

The foundation gave small grants to a wide variety of civic initiatives that were independent of the prevailing party-state mechanism. We provided support to experimental schools, libraries, amateur theatrical companies, the zither players' association, farmers' clubs and other voluntary social organizations, artists and art exhibitions, and cultural and research projects. We carefully calibrated our activities so that the programs that would be considered constructive by the government outweighed those that would be regarded with suspicion by the authorities in charge of ideology. The idea was to break the monopoly of the party-state: The falsehood of the prevailing party dogma would become apparent when an alternative was available. The idea worked. With a $3 million budget, the foundation provided an effective alternative to the Ministries of Culture and Education, which had vastly greater resources.

The foundation was exempt from the limitations and negative side effects that afflict other foundations. Civil society adopted the foundation as its own and took good care of it. We did not have to exercise controls; civil society did it for us. For example, when we wanted to give a grant to an association of the blind for talking books, somebody warned us that the organization was corrupt. The tip-off enabled us to avoid being taken advantage of. I visited Hungary often; and whenever we decided on a course of action, the next time I visited, I found the decision miraculously translated into reality.

Encouraged by the success of the Hungarian foundation, I ventured further afield. By 1987, I had set up foundations inside Poland, China, and the Soviet Union. The foundations in Poland and the Soviet Union succeeded, but the one in China failed. In the Soviet Union, I took my cue that something had changed when Mikhail Gorbachev telephoned Andrei Sakharov, who was in exile in Gorky, in December 1986 and asked him to "resume his patriotic activities in Moscow." (Sakharov told me later that the telephone line had to be installed the night before especially for the occasion.) If it had been business as usual he would have been sent abroad.

I went to Moscow in early March 1987 as a tourist, and ended up setting up a foundation on the Hungarian model with the Cultural Foundation of the USSR as my partner. The Cultural Foundation was a newly formed organization, and Raisa Gorbachev was its patron. Our joint venture was called Cultural Initiative. I was hoping that Andrei Sakharov would be my personal representative, but he refused. "Your money will go to fill the coffers of the KGB," he told me. I am proud to have proved him wrong.

In China, I went into partnership with an institute that was promoting economic reform. Our main activity was providing scholarships for study abroad. The idea of awarding grants on the basis of merit was an alien concept. People who received support felt obliged to the provider; moreover, they felt that the provider was obliged to them because the provider's reputation depended on the success or failure of its grantees. I called this attitude "feudalism of the mind." The foundation was caught up in a power struggle within the party. Normally, dozens of relevant authorities have to sign off on a new initiative; for this one, the joint venture was authorized by the sole signature of Bao Tong, an aide to the general secretary of the party, Zhao Ziyang. This attracted the attention of the internal security organs and they used the foundation to attack him and his patron, Zhao Ziyang. To protect himself, Bao Tong transferred the foundation to the direction of the external security organs, which removed the foundation from the purview of the internal organs. When I discovered that the foundation was effectively run by the political police, I closed it just before the Tiananmen Square massacre. Regrettably, Bao Tong ended up in jail.

As the Soviet empire disintegrated, I continued to set up foundations in other countries. By 1991, I had a network of foundations covering more that twenty countries. I never bothered to explain what I meant by open society. People understood instinctively that it meant the opposite of the closed society from which they wanted to free themselves.

OPERATING IN
FAR-FROM-EQUILIBRIUM CONDITIONS

This was a revolutionary period, not only for the countries of the former Soviet empire, but also for me and my foundation network. I considered myself a specialist in far-from-equilibrium situations. My father had taught me that at the height of a revolution, practically anything is possible. The first man who walks into a plant manager's office, he told me, can take over the plant; the next man already finds somebody in charge. Armed with this insight, I was determined to be the first man. I was in a unique position to accomplish this. I had political convictions, financial means, and an understanding of the importance of the moment. Many people had one or two of these attributes, but I was unique in having all three. I felt duty-bound to devote all my energies to the work of the foundations. Other Western foundations moved so slowly that it took them years to overcome the legal obstacles; I plowed ahead without paying much attention to legal niceties. In the Soviet Union, we started functioning two years ahead of other foundations, and we had the field to ourselves. We established foundations in Estonia, Lithuania and Ukraine even before they became independent. The Central European University, which was meant to serve as an intellectual resource center to the foundation network, started giving graduate courses even before it was accredited—the first students received their degrees retroactively. We operated without a plan or a budget during this period of explosive growth. We embarked on numerous new initiatives, but we cut them off if they did not live up to expectations; and when they had fulfilled their mission, we terminated them. Our annual expenditures jumped from $3 million to more than $300 million within three years. This would not have been possible if we had operated in a more conventional manner.

We engaged in a wide range of activities. In a transition from a totalitarian system to an open society everything needs to be done at once, and in many areas we were practically the only source of support. We were ready to back almost any project if we could identify people, either inside or outside the country, on whom we could rely to carry it out. Because the dollar went a long way in that part of the world, we became involved in a myriad of projects. The whole was greater than the sum of the parts: taken together, the projects had a significant social and political impact in fostering open societies. Occasionally, we made some very large grants; we called them "mega-projects." For instance, I allocated $100 million to preserve and reform Soviet science. This was a time of hyperinflation and $500 was enough for a family to live on for a year. The International Science Foundation gave out more than 25,000 emergency grants to the most prominent scientists selected by a simple and transparent method: three citations in an internationally recognized journal was the criterion. The $500 grants were paid in dollars. That cost less than $20 million. The rest of the money went for research projects selected by peer review in which leading scientists from all over the world participated. The scheme was attacked in the Russian parliament, but it was vociferously defended by the scientists. The Duma eventually passed a vote of thanks.

I focused my energies on setting up the foundations, selecting the boards that were to be entrusted with spending my money, and addressing the larger issues of economic and political reform. As early as 1988, I proposed setting up a market-oriented open sector within the Soviet Union that would be implanted within the body of the centrally planned economy. The Soviet authorities responded positively and a series of high-level meetings were held until it became clear that the centrally planned economy was already too weak to nurture a market economy. Later, I became intimately involved in the so-called Shatalin Plan, which sought to replace the Soviet Union with an economic union among independent states; and I shepherded a Soviet delegation, led by Grigory Yavlinsky, through the 1991 annual meeting of the World Bank and International Monetary Fund (IMF), during which they tried—in vain—to gather international support. In Poland, I advocated and supported the Big Bang—a sudden transition to a market economy—that was introduced on January 1, 1990. Subsequently, I prevailed on the Hungarian government to convoke a meeting exploring how the Comecon (an international trade agreement among Communist countries) could be reorganized along market-oriented lines, again without success.*

As a general rule, whenever a task could be accomplished with my foundation's resources alone, it got done; whenever it involved persuading policymakers or institutions, it ran aground. For instance, when Leonid Kuchma was elected president of Ukraine, I was able to provide him with advisors who helped Ukraine obtain an IMF program within a few weeks; when I tried to persuade the IMF to earmark its assistance to Russia for the payment of pensions and unemployment benefits, I failed.

I became intimately involved in the affairs of the Russian state during Boris Yeltsin's presidency. I watched at close quarters, but did not participate in, the infamous Loan for Shares scheme. I did participate in the first auction in which the state received real money: the privatization of Svyazinvest, the state telephone company. I did so in the belief that robber capitalism was about to give way to legitimate capitalism. I was wrong, and my purchase turned into the worst investment decision of my career. The robber capitalists fell

*For a more detailed account, see my *Opening The Soviet System* (London: Weidenfeld and Nicolson, 1990; privately republished, 2000), or *Underwriting Democracy* (New York: PublicAffairs, 2004).

out with one another and engaged in a no-holds-barred fight among themselves. The egregious deals and corruption I witnessed defies the imagination.

APPLYING THE FRAMEWORK

During all this time, I was guided by the conceptual framework I outlined earlier. In my 1990 book, *Opening the Soviet System*, I combined the static models of open and closed societies with my theory of reflexivity to provide an interpretation of the rise and fall of the Soviet system. To do so, I introduced an interesting modification to the boom-bust theory that models an initially self-reinforcing, but eventually self-defeating, process of change. I applied the same approach to the absence of change. I justified it by arguing that changelessness, instead of being an expression of equilibrium, is also a condition of disequilibrium characterized by a large gap between prevailing perceptions and actual conditions, and that there is a reflexive interaction between them. My contention was that changelessness can also take an initially self-reinforcing, but eventually self-defeating, course. Here is an extract:

In a closed society the prevailing dogma is far removed from reality, but the system is viable as long as there is a way to adjust the dogma when it gets too far out of line with reality. A totalitarian regime needs a totalitarian at the top. Stalin fulfilled that role with gusto. He enforced the dogma but also changed it when necessary. Under him the system attained its maximum extension, in both ideological and territorial coverage. There was hardly an aspect of existence that escaped its influence. Even genetics obeyed Stalinist doctrine. Not every science could be subjugated with equal success, but at least the scientists could be tamed and their contact with youth restricted by confining them in the Institutes of the Academy and preventing them from teaching at universities. Terror played a large part in making the system work but the cover of ideology successfully concealed the underlying coercion and fear.

It is a testimony to Stalin's genius that the system survived him by some thirty-five years. There was a brief moment of hope when Khrushchev revealed some of the truth about Stalin in his speech before the Twentieth Congress but, eventually, the hierarchy reasserted itself. This was the period when dogma was preserved by administrative methods, without any belief in its validity. As long as there had been a live totalitarian at the helm, the system enjoyed some maneuverability: the party line could be changed at the whim of the dictator and the previous one excised. Now that flexibility was lost and the system became as rigid as my theoretical model prescribes. At the same time a subtle process of decay set in. Every enterprise and institution sought to improve its own position. Since none of them had any autonomy, they had to barter whatever powers they had for the resources they needed for their own survival. Gradually an elaborate system of institutional bargaining replaced the central planning and central control that had prevailed while the system had been in totalitarian hands. Moreover, an informal system of economic relationships evolved which supplemented and filled the gaps left by the formal system.

The inadequacy of the system because increasingly evident and the pressure for reform mounted.

I went on to argue that reform accelerates the process of disintegration. It introduces or legitimizes alternatives at a time when the system depends on the lack of alternatives for its survival. Alternatives raise questions; they undermine authority; they not only reveal discrepancies in the existing arrangements but reinforce them by diverting resources to more profitable uses. A command economy cannot avoid a misallocation of resources: Introduce a modicum of choice and the shortages are bound to become more pronounced. Moreover, the profits that can be earned by diverting resources from the command economy are much greater than what can be earned from productive activity; it is therefore not at all certain that overall production will benefit.

As a consequence, I argued, the Soviet Union was in a state of total disintegration. All aspects of the system were affected, its ideology, its morality, its government, its economy, and the territorial empire. When the system had been intact, all these elements were integrated; now that the system was falling apart, the elements were decaying in various ways and at various speeds, but events in one area tended to reinforce developments in the others. I gave a prescient account of the ensuing chaotic conditions that was based on this analysis.

PROMOTING OPEN SOCIETY

At the same time as I was writing *Opening the Soviet System*, I was putting into practice my ideas about open society.

My foundations were expanding by leaps and bounds. There was no plan, not even a budget. We proceeded on the basis of trial and error. This method had a downside: We made a lot of errors. As a result, the foundations got caught up in the turmoil in which they sought to act as a guide. This was particularly true in Russia. Just before the August 1991 putsch that briefly deposed Gorbachev, I had to organize a putsch within the foundation to regain control. Unfortunately, the people who helped me in the putsch also got out of control, so I had to organize a second putsch to remove them. These events caused us to lose valuable time at a critical moment in Russian history.

My goal was to make my foundations into a prototype of open society, but I realized that this ambition was a fertile fallacy. An open society has to be self-sustaining, but the foundations depended on my financial support for their survival. In reality, the foundations played the role of deus ex-machina; but it takes a deus ex-machina to alter the course of history. An open society is a more sophisticated, more advanced form of social organization than a closed society. A closed society requires only a single interpretation of reality: the one embodied in the prevailing party-state dogma. In an open society, every citizen is required to form his or her own view of the world, and society needs institutions that allow people with different views and interests to live together in peace. The task is so immense that it is impossible to make the transition from closed to open society in one step without a helping hand from the outside. It was this insight that drove me to devote all my energies and resources to providing such a helping hand, exactly because my insight was not widely shared. Regrettably, the West failed to rise to the occasion. As a result, the transition was never accomplished in most of the former Soviet Union.

REVISING THE FRAMEWORK

I have not changed my opinion about the failure of the international community to provide assistance, but in other respects I was forced by my experiences to undertake a major revision of my conceptual framework. The framework treated open and closed society as alternatives. The lesson I learned was that the collapse of a closed society does not automatically lead to an open society; it may lead to continuing collapse and disintegration that is followed by some kind of restoration or stabilization. Thus a simple dichotomy between open and closed society is inadequate.

Open society is endangered not only by dogmatic ideologies and totalitarian regimes but also by a breakdown of society and failed states. Stephen Holmes, a political scientist who worked with my Russian foundation, put it well in his article: "What Russia Teaches Us Now: How Weak States Threaten Freedom."* This was new. Popper considered only totalitarian ideologies enemies of the open society. My original framework recognized that too much liberty and a deficiency of purpose may make dogmatic ideologies attractive; but it left out of account the possibility that the breakdown of a closed society may not give rise to an open society but to further disintegration. Instead of treating open and closed soci-

*Stephen Holmes, "What Russia Teaches Us Now: How Weak States Threaten Freedom," *American Prospect* (July-August 1997): 3039.

ety as alternatives, I had to reposition open society as being threatened from both directions: too much liberty, anarchy, and failed states on the one hand; dogmatic ideologies and authoritarian or totalitarian regimes of all kinds on the other. Open society came to occupy a precious middle ground that was endangered by extremes of all kinds.

This construction fits in well with the modified boom-bust theory I used to account for the rise and fall of the Soviet system: Open society constitutes near-equilibrium conditions precariously poised between the static disequilibrium of a closed society and the dynamic disequilibrium of chaos and disorientation. Equilibrium in this context denotes a correspondence between reality and its perception. Near-equilibrium is superior to far-from-equilibrium conditions because it enables participants better to cope with reality than they could if their views were far removed from reality. The participants may not agree with this judgment: They may prefer to be deluded; but in any contest, those whose understanding is closer to reality have a better chance of prevailing.

This tripartite division between static disequilibrium, near-equilibrium, and dynamic disequilibrium may be compared to the three states of water: frozen, liquid, and gaseous. Closed society is rigid, open society is fluid, and revolution chaotic. The analogy is far-fetched, but it serves as a graphic illustration. The tripartite division is more complicated than a dichotomy, but it incorporates the lesson taught by the disintegration of the Soviet system.

If we have to abandon the dichotomy between open and closed, why use the term "open society" to describe liberal democracies? It will be recalled that it was almost by accident that Karl Popper's book was titled *The Open Society and*

Its Enemies. Out of that accident, open society has come to denote near-equilibrium conditions. The term "open society" is certainly more user-friendly than "near-equilibrium conditions," but "liberal democracy" may be more exact. "Liberal democracy" is a term widely used in an international context, although "liberal" has become something of a term of opprobrium in domestic politics. Open society does not carry the ideological baggage attached to the word "liberal." I intend to stick to it because I consider the epistemological argument behind it important, not to mention all the activities of my foundations that have been carried out under that name.

Open society means almost the same thing as liberal democracy, but it implies an elaborate conceptual framework that is not necessarily part of the concept of liberal democracy. Open society derives the need for liberal democracy from the recognition of our imperfect understanding or fallibility. This is not obvious from the expression "open society." It needs to be made explicit by stating the argument. At the same time, the term "open society" describes a society that is open to the outside; this society allows the free flow of goods, ideas and people. "Open society" also describes a society that is open on the inside, a society that allows freedom of thought and social mobility. As a descriptive term, "open society" is self-explanatory, but the epistemological analysis behind it requires an explanation. I have gone through this long historical account to provide it.

THE NEXT CHALLENGE

The modified framework that currently serves as my conceptual guide is exposed to significant challenges. This forces me into further rethinking; but instead of considering the challenges on the level of timelessly valid generalizations, I shall treat them as problems that confront us (humanity in general, and me and my foundation network in particular) at the present moment in history. This is the approach I follow in most of my books. To expect a conceptual framework to be both timelessly valid and applicable to current conditions would contradict the postulate of imperfect understanding or fallibility—not only my postulate of radical fallibility but Karl Popper's more modest contention that we *may* be wrong. As a participant, I cannot avoid giving expression to my biases. If I claimed for my opinions the same kind of timeless validity that I claim for my conceptual framework it would invalidate the framework. Moreover, my framework does not claim to be comprehensive. For instance, it lacks any consideration of power relations. Therefore, it cannot serve as the basis for arriving at practical judgments.

The challenge that preoccupies me emanates from an unexpected source: the United States. Who would have thought that the oldest, most well-established, and most powerful open society in the world could pose a threat not only to the concept of open society at home but also to peace and stability in the world? Yet that is what has happened in the aftermath of the terrorist attack of 9/11. In my previous book, I tried to pin the blame on the Bush administration. *The Bubble of American Supremacy* was a passionate political polemic in which I argued that by rejecting George W. Bush in the presidential elections of 2004 we would repudiate his policies. We could then attribute the excesses of the Bush administration since 9/11—which I compared to the later stages of a stock market bubble—to a temporary aberration brought about by the traumatic experience of 9/11 and then skillfully exploited by an ill-intentioned leadership. But that is not what happened. President Bush was reelected. I must now pose the question: What is wrong with us as a society? I shall explore this question in Part 2 of this book. The conceptual framework I have presented will be helpful in answering the question because it identifies some of the flaws that are inherent in an open society. That is my justification for having taken the reader on such a strenuous journey.

My concern is not only with the United States but with the world at large. The United States is the dominant power in the world today. It sets the agenda and the rest of the world has to respond. But the Bush administration has set the wrong agenda. It is difficult to identify exactly what it is because it is made up of various themes, but it is not difficult to establish that it is taking the world in the wrong direction. The survival of the fittest is a major theme, and competition, not cooperation, is supposed to determine who is the fittest. This is the wrong approach, however; our globalized world is not a jungle ruled by naked power. There is some order in the world, and how that order works depends greatly on how the dominant power behaves.

Globalization has made the world increasingly interdependent. Mankind faces challenges that can be met only through increased cooperation. The United States is not all-powerful, as we have discovered to great cost in Iraq, but little can be done in the way of international cooperation without the leadership of the United States, or at least its active participation. This places a special obligation on the United States to show concern for the well-being of the world as a whole. The rest of the world does not have a vote in Congress, but it is Washington that decides the fate of the world. In this respect, the situation is reminiscent of the time when America was a British colony and subject to taxation without representation. Now that the United States has become the imperial power, it bears a unique responsibility for the future of the world.

In discussing the problems of the prevailing world order, my conceptual framework is of limited use. It does explain why mankind's ability to govern itself has not kept pace with its ability to exploit nature—it has to do with reflexivity—but it cannot provide a blueprint for global governance. My framework is built on an insight into the relationships between thinking and reality and it does not constitute a comprehensive view of the world. It is particularly ill-suited to deal with relationships of power. Nevertheless, we cannot avoid the issues of global governance. I have dealt with them in the past—particularly in my book *Open Society: Reforming Global Capitalism*. Part 2 of this work serves as a revision and an updating of that book in the light of recent developments. Although I speak of a global open society, it is more obvious to me now than it was at the time I wrote the previous book that I am discussing a political project and not an epistemological one.

PART II

The Present Moment
in History

CHAPTER 3

What's Wrong With America?

PERSONAL INVOLVEMENT

What is wrong with America? I should like to approach the question in a circuitous way by examining my foundation's programs in the United States. This will establish a link with my conceptual framework and maintain the continuity of the narrative.

My foundation became active in the United States in the early 1990s. By then, the disintegration of the Soviet system had run its course and order had begun to emerge from the chaos. This applied both to the countries concerned and to the foundation network. But the new regimes left much to be desired, and the foundation network continued to have a full agenda. Nevertheless, the activities were not as all-absorbing as they had been during the period of turmoil. This allowed me to turn my attention to the problems of globalization. I also extended the foundation network to other parts of the world, particularly Africa, but I did not forget the United States. The network became truly global in scope.

Open society is an imperfect society that holds itself open

to improvement. Applying this definition, I could detect several imperfections in American society that would lend themselves to improvement. In particular, I identified two insoluble problems where our ways of dealing with them made matters worse rather than better: death and drugs. These were among the first issues my U.S. foundation addressed.

Death is a fact of life, but our society resists accepting it as such. People go to great lengths to deny death or to ignore it. The medical profession often goes too far in prolonging life, and Medicare does not even recognize dying as a reimbursable medical event. All this renders the process of dying far more painful than it needs to be. I set up the Project on Death in America, which was devoted to reducing the pain associated with death. The project tapped into the considerable professional expertise that was available on the subject and made it more widely available—mainly by establishing fellowships and spreading the word among professionals and the general public. Contrary to the accusations of my right-wing opponents, the project did not advocate euthanasia; it advocated end-of-life care. It has been so successful in carrying out its mission that after a one-time extension of its original five-year life span, it was terminated. The principles of end-of-life care have been firmly established for the medical profession and, to an increasing extent, for the general public. The fear or denial of death has not disappeared. As we shall see, it has played an important role in the war on terror, and it resurfaced notably in the Terri Schiavo case, but these manifestations are more on the political than the professional level and they need to be treated accordingly.

Drug addiction is another insoluble problem, and the war

on drugs makes the problem worse. This was the thesis that got me involved in the drug problem. Drug policy is eminently suitable for practicing the principles of open society— the ultimate solution is beyond our reach and the pursuit of a "drug-free America" is liable to be counterproductive. I had no firm views on what to do about America's drug abuse problem, but as a disciple of Popper I thought we may be able to improve the situation through a process of trial and error. What I knew for sure was that the war on drugs was doing more harm than good and that we had to explore ways to reduce the harm that drug addiction causes. That was the approach I advocated under the name of "harm reduction." By "harm," I meant not only drug addiction but also the harm caused by the war on drugs: the high rates of incarceration; the disruption of African American and Hispanic communities; the producing countries turning into narco-states, and corruption and abuse of power. I found myself enmeshed in a problem area in which prejudice and intolerance are at their worst. Drug policy reform is an arena that few people are willing to enter. Politicians regard it as the third rail—touch it and you die. Being independently wealthy, I considered myself in a better position to take a stand than most people. But I did not fully appreciate the vituperative opposition I would encounter, nor did I anticipate the war on terror, which shares so many similarities with the war on drugs.

When I took a stand against the reelection of President Bush, my stand on drugs made me more vulnerable to attack. I have been accused of many things, from being the "Daddy Warbucks" of drug legalization (Joseph Califano, the former health, education, and welfare secretary) to a financier of the drug trade (Dennis Hastert, Speaker of the House). But once engaged, I did not withdraw. I supported efforts to reform draconian sanctions such as the Rockefeller drug laws in New York, and became, during the late 1990s, the leading private funder of needle exchange programs to stem the spread of HIV/AIDS. I also joined with others to fund state ballot initiatives to legalize marijuana for medical purposes, to require treatment instead of incarceration for drug possession, and to curtail the excessive asset forfeiture powers of police and prosecutors. And I supported the creation of a national organization, the Drug Policy Alliance, to advocate for harm reduction practices and principles. The battle is ongoing.

I found open society endangered in the United States by another tendency: activities that used to be regarded as professions were turning into businesses. This applied to professions such as law and medicine—not to mention politics. When professions turn into businesses focused on profit, professional standards become endangered; this, in turn, reinforces the deficiency in values that is characteristic of open societies. My concern was derived directly from my conceptual framework. It led me to set up projects on law and medicine as professions. The projects then took on a life of their own and they engaged in various worthwhile activities, but they did not make much headway in solving the problem that led to their establishment. Criminal justice turned out to be the field in which the U.S. foundation really showed its mettle, partly because of the human rights and civil liberties background of its leadership and partly because there is so much to be done.

But the lack of respect for professional values has become even more pronounced than it was when we embarked on our projects and now extends beyond the professions to science and academia. Intellectual property rights have turned thought into property. Research is conducted with a view to generating wealth rather than pure knowledge and academia is losing its sense of identity as an end in itself. The chase after intellectual property rights inhibits the pursuit of truth.

To make matters worse, both science and academia have come under ideologically motivated attack. In science, the advocates of intelligent design have exploited the tolerance for alternative hypotheses by claiming equal time for their non-scientific theory; in academia, a right wing group has capitalized on the striving for better racial and gender balance to agitate for political diversity, thereby introducing party politics into academic hiring. Universities find it hard to resist because racial and gender quotas have weakened their case for hiring exclusively on merit.

Just as a business mentality has entered areas in which it does not properly belong, now politics is doing the same. Both tendencies endanger open society. The foundation has a new task ahead.

Although my foundation addressed some of the weak points of American society, I considered America safe and solid as a democracy. I did not get deeply involved in party politics, although I had a natural leaning towards the Democratic Party. I had many dealings with the Clinton administration, but mainly on issues of foreign policy. On the drug issue, I found the Democrats no better than the Republicans— indeed, I made common cause with conservative Republicans such as George Shultz, a former secretary of state, and libertarians such as Milton Friedman and the Cato Institute, although I disagreed with them on other issues.

I stood for a more interventionist policy in the Yugoslav civil war, in order to put an end to the violations of human rights that were taking place. At Christmas 1992, I announced a $50 million donation for the purpose of providing humanitarian aid to besieged Sarajevo. The idea was that if humanitarian groups became involved under the aegis of the UNHCR, the UN would have to give them military protection. The idea did not work, but the humanitarian assistance, brilliantly orchestrated by that genius of relief operations, Fred Cuny (who later perished in Chechnya), did make a significant contribution to the survival of Sarajevo. I joined a bipartisan group, the Action Council for Peace in the Balkans, which urged the Clinton administration to take a more aggressive stance on Bosnia. Paul Wolfowitz was also a member of the group, and together we used to lobby Secretary of State Madeleine Albright. I also supported NATO (North Atlantic Treaty Organization) intervention in Kosovo.

Then came the election of President George W. Bush in 2000 and the terrorist attacks on September 11, 2001. I felt that open society was endangered in the United States—not so much because of the terrorist attacks but because of the way President Bush responded to them. He claimed that September 11, 2001, changed everything and that was a self-fulfilling prophecy. By declaring war on terror, he suspended the critical mode of thinking that is at the core of an open society. Criticism of the president's policies was denounced as unpatriotic. Congress passed the U.S.A. PATRIOT Act* without even having time to read it and authorized the President to use force. President Bush proceeded to invade Iraq

*U.S.A. PATRIOT stands for "Uniting and Strengthening America by Providing Appropriate Tools Required to Intercept and Obstruct Terrorism."

under false pretenses. When the most powerful nation on earth distorts the truth, disregards world opinion, and flouts international law, the world order is in great peril.

These developments came as a surprise to me. Who would have thought that the United States, which I had learned to regard as the champion of democracy and open society, could become a threat to the world order? Having exerted myself in promoting the ideas of open society abroad, I felt honor-bound to do the same at home. I propounded my views in *The Bubble of American Supremacy*, and then I looked for ways to put my money where my mouth was. I became as deeply engaged in trying to remove President Bush from the White House as I had been in trying to help the countries of the former Soviet empire to make the transition from a closed to an open society.

I commissioned two political experts to advise me about what I could do to oppose the reelection of President Bush. They both came up with the same plan. There was a grass-roots voter mobilization effort planned for five battleground states; if it could be extended to all sixteen states in play that could make a tangible difference to the outcome. I brought together a small number of other donors and we pledged enough money to get it started. Subsequently, we acted as catalysts in attracting financial support from others. I also put my mouth where my money went: In the final stages of the elections, I embarked on a speaking tour and advertised my views in double-paged spreads in the *Wall Street Journal* and other newspapers.

It was a new departure for me to become involved in partisan politics, and it was not a congenial one. Not surprisingly, the Republican National Committee identified me as an enemy and proceeded to unleash a concerted propaganda campaign against me. This gave me a first-hand experience of the kind of distortions political campaigns entail. I did not like it, but I considered it a price worth paying because the stakes were so high. Nothing else I could do would benefit the world as much as helping to limit President Bush to one term.

It did not happen. President Bush was reelected with an unquestionable majority. Strangely enough, I was not devastated because I felt I had done everything I could to prevent it. But I felt obliged to rethink and to regroup. I could no longer pin the blame on the Bush administration; the American electorate had endorsed its policies. I had to face the question: What's wrong with America? What's wrong with us? That is the question I want to address here. But before I do so, I have to consider a possible objection: In less than two years after President Bush's reelection, public opinion has turned against him and the invasion of Iraq. Perhaps it is not the electorate that is at fault; perhaps the elections came just a little too soon, before the unpleasant realities could sink in. I wish I could think so, but reality militates against it. The American public has turned against the war in Iraq, but it still subscribes to the war on terror. Since I firmly believe that it is with the war on terror that America went wrong and entered far-from-equilibrium territory, I cannot accept that we have fully returned to our senses until we have renounced the war on terror. So the question stands. I shall explain at greater length in the next chapter why I think the war on terror has made us less secure.

APPLYING THE CONCEPTUAL FRAMEWORK

An examination of what is wrong with America today has to start with an appeal to the open society model in my conceptual framework. Although the model is meant to be abstract and timelessly valid, it is remarkably relevant to the United States. That is not really surprising because I had the United States in mind when I wrote the book in the early 1960s. I had recently moved to New York from London, and my description of a brave new world based on transactions and contracts rather than on personal relationships reflected my first impressions of America. I remember looking at the identical houses of Levittown and other suburbs and imagining that husbands could easily go home to the wrong wives. The important point is that the model was constructed in the early 1960s, so that if it is relevant to conditions today, those conditions must have roots that go deeper than the current administration.

The model stressed the uncertainty inherent in the critical mode of thinking and pointed out that the individual is a weak reed on which to base the values of a society. If fear, uncertainty, and the deficiency of purpose that characterizes an open society become unbearable burdens, then a charismatic leader offering a dogmatic mode of thinking may appear as the salvation.

I had this model in mind when I wrote *The Bubble of American Supremacy*. I argued that the Bush administration was exploiting the terrorist attack of 9/11 to install fear in the public mind and to gain uncritical acceptance for policies that were endangering open society at home and threatening peace and stability in the world. I invoked the boom-bust theory I had developed in the financial markets to show that the Bush administration's vain and eventually counterproductive pursuit of American supremacy had the characteristics of a bubble. Although previous mistakes in American policy were within the bounds of normalcy and remained subject to critical examination, 9/11, in the words of President Bush, "changed everything"; and that is when we entered far-from-equilibrium territory. Criticism was declared unpatriotic, and the checks and balances that safeguard our democracy were removed. The war on terror enabled the president to assume unlimited executive powers and to mislead the nation into an ill-conceived and ill-executed adventure that would undermine the American supremacy that it was meant to underpin.

The conclusions in *The Bubble of American Supremacy* were borne out by subsequent events. Nevertheless, by venting its ire on the Bush administration, the book failed to answer the question I am now forced to pose: What is wrong with us? I hope to answer it by exploring in greater detail how my abstract conceptual framework applies to the specific circumstances of today.

Let me be more specific. I watched events unfold after 9/11 with a bias rooted in my adolescent experience of Nazism and communism. My conceptual framework was also based on that experience. When I heard President Bush say, "Either you are with us or you are with the terrorists," I was reminded of Nazi propaganda. I said so in an interview with the *Washington Post* that turned out to be counterproductive. It allowed the conservative propaganda machine to assert that I had called Bush a Nazi and to label me as an extremist at a time when I was trying to label *them* as extremists. The tactics employed by the Republican National Committee (RNC) and its handmaidens were also reminiscent of Nazi and Communist propaganda. They painted a totally false picture of me and what I stood for, yet they established it in the public mind by constant repetition. But that is a side issue. Is it valid to compare the Bush administration to the Nazi and Communist regimes? That is the question I am asking when I say I need to explore how my framework relates to the current situation.

An Invidious Comparison

There is one major difference that overshadows all the others: The United States is a functioning democracy with an independent judiciary and the rule of law. Nazi Germany and the Soviet Union were totalitarian dictatorships. Only when we look beyond this glaring contrast does the question become interesting because then we can discern some surprising similarities along with the differences.

Let me start with the similarities. First, there are similarities in the lifestyles of the Weimar Republic and the United States in the aftermath of the Vietnam War and leading up to the war on terror: The unbridled pursuit of self-interest and self-indulgence to the detriment of morality and traditional values caused a revulsion in both societies. In Germany, which suffered from the consequences of the Versailles Treaty and hyperinflation, the revulsion took the form of national socialism; in the United States, it manifested itself in the rise of religious fundamentalism which until recently stayed at the fringes of politics.

Second, the Bush administration and the Nazi and Communist regimes all engaged in the politics of fear. The 9/11 attacks had their counterpart in the Reichstag Fire in Germany and the Kirov murder in the Soviet Union. I am not subscribing to conspiracy theories; I take all three events as exogenous happenings that the governments exploited for their own purposes. The attacks of 9/11 were by far the most traumatic of these events.

Third, in Nazi Germany, the Soviet Union, and present-day America, political life came to be dominated by a movement that originated outside the parliamentary system and seized state power. In Russia, the Communists captured the state by revolution. In Weimar Germany, the Nazis formed a political party and came to power through a constitutional route. In the United States, the conservative movement first captured the Republican Party, then gained control of Congress and the presidency.

Not all movements that originate outside the parliamentary system pose a threat to open society. Take for instance the Green movement in Europe. The reason the comparison is relevant is that once a movement comes to power it is endowed with the authority and respectability of the state. Actions and policies that would otherwise be considered illegitimate are accepted as legitimate. Challenging them is tantamount to challenging the symbolic significance of the State. That is why I am treading on such treacherous grounds when I am drawing this invidious comparison. The symbolic significance of the State is even greater in the United States with its deep democratic traditions than it was in Germany or the Soviet Union. But that is where this similarity ends. With the capture of the executive power of the state, the Nazis and the Russian Communists could establish totalitarian dictatorships. That is where the United States is different because of the rule of law and well-established democratic institutions. Even so, some of the actions and policies of the Bush administration do pose a threat to our open society and our respect for the state should not blind us to them. Without going into details about specific actions that may be extra-legal, I want to point out the systemic challenge: President Bush is claiming the unlimited extension of executive power in the war on terror and has appointed judges to the Supreme Court who support this view.

Finally, there are the similarities in propaganda methods. Indeed, the Bush administration has been able to improve on the techniques used by the Nazi and the Communist propaganda machines by drawing on the innovations of the advertising and marketing industries. There is now a scientific basis for manipulating opinion and behavior. As noted, cognitive science has made great strides in recent years in understanding how the human mind functions. People can be more easily influenced by an appeal to their emotions than by rational arguments; but, to be effective, the emotional appeal must not be brought into sharp focus. It is eerie how successful the Bush administration has been in using Orwellian newspeak. Every time I hear traces of this newspeak, I suffer an allergic reaction. Why does the general public not react in the same way? Why is the public so tone-deaf?

There is a related question that I find equally troubling. In Orwell's *1984*, the Ministry of Truth exercised full control over the media. In today's America, the right-wing propaganda machine does not enjoy a similar monopoly, yet it has been able to impose its interpretation of reality with remarkable success. How is that possible? It is almost as if people were clamoring to be deceived.

Before I try to answer these questions, I need to consider some of the differences between the Bush administration and totalitarian ideologies such as national socialism, fascism, and communism—apart from the obvious one that the United States is very far from being a totalitarian dictatorship. It is noteworthy that the Bush administration is not guided by a comprehensive ideology. We can discern several strands of ideology, but they do not add up to an all-embracing interpretation of reality. In *The Bubble of American Supremacy*, I identified three major schools of thought, and I even tried to weave them into a comprehensive worldview; but the attempt was less than convincing mainly because the adherents of one strand do not necessarily subscribe to the other strands. The three schools of thought were market fundamentalism, religious fundamentalism, and the neoconservative advocacy of American supremacy. I identified the unifying theme as social Darwinism, in which life is a competition for the survival of the fittest, survival being decided by competition, not cooperation. It fitted market fundamentalism and the neoconservative attitude, but it failed to account for religious fundamentalism. It would be tempting to speak of religious nationalism as the dominant ideology because there is a strong nationalist theme in Bush policies, but that would leave market fundamentalists out in the cold. Forcing a unified ideology on the supporters of the Bush administration just does not work. This leads me to the conclusion that the current regime has the support of disparate groups unified only by the desire for political power and influence.

I witnessed the coalition at work when I participated in one of the famous Wednesday-morning meetings organized by Grover Norquist. The meeting was attended by representatives of the conservative movement, ranging from the Heritage Foundation to the *Washington Times*. It was a fascinating experience. Norquist conducted the meeting with iron discipline. The room was filled to capacity; many people were standing, but those who ranked highest were seated at the table, and the second highest had seats along the wall. Everybody spoke faster than normal, and fully sixty items were dealt with in the space of an hour. Speakers made concise presentations; people volunteered to support others in the expectation that others would support them in return. On the occasion I attended, the items presented included individuals seeking support for their electoral races or a new book, an emissary of the White House reaffirming support for John Bolton's nomination, and lobbyists arguing for various legislative proposals. The distinction between the public interest and private interests was blurred. If there was a dominant theme, it was to reduce taxes and regulations by all possible means, but it was clear that this could be accomplished only by hand washing hand. I was told that similar Wednesday meetings took place across the country.

After the regular meeting, I was invited to address the gathering, and that was the strangest part of the day. My remarks, in which I did not mince words, were surprisingly well-received, and several participants were eager to explore how we could cooperate on particular issues. Obviously, they believed in building coalitions, and they did not think of themselves as evil. When I spoke of a nefarious right-wing conspiracy that was well-represented in the room, they let it pass as if it did not refer to them. Their self-confidence amazed me, and I did not hesitate to say so. I found the group truly impressive; there is nothing like it on the opposite side.

In evaluating the similarities and differences between the Bush administration and totalitarian ideologies, one sees that the differences far outweigh the similarities. There is nothing totalitarian about the United States, and the Bush administration does not even have a clear-cut ideology. So the comparison with the Nazi and Communist regimes is far-fetched. Yet there are enough similarities to indicate that open society is endangered in some ways that do not quite fit into my conceptual framework. Instead of fitting the threat into the framework, I need to understand the nature of the threat and, if necessary, modify the framework.

THE FAILURES OF LEADERSHIP

Over the past two years, the nature of the threat posed by the Bush administration has become more clearly defined: It consists of the undue extension of executive powers. That is the most significant similarity with the Nazi and Communist regimes, although this is not immediately obvious because Germany and Russia did not enjoy the same division of powers to start with as the United States.

It has also become clear that the threat emanates more from Vice President Dick Cheney than from the president himself. George W. Bush is more like an unwitting tool; Cheney is the power behind the throne. Now that his policies have come under attack, the vice president has defended them; and that is how his true character has been revealed. People who knew Cheney before he became vice president speak highly of him, adding perhaps, "He is not the Cheney I used to know." By contrast, I have always seen him as a paranoid, Strangelove kind of character. Cheney and Rumsfeld have largely succeeded in imposing their views on the Bush administration. Now they are beleaguered, but they refuse to yield. Their rhetoric is as shrill as ever and they resist any encroachment on their powers. They threatened to have the President veto the legislation that outlaws torture, and when the new law was approved by a veto-proof majority, they managed to introduce an amendment that attempts to exempt prisoners at Guantanamo from the reach of American courts.

The Failures of Followership

Instead of embellishing my indictment of the leadership, I shall focus on the character of the followership because that is where, in my opinion, the threat to open society lies. The American public has shown a remarkable indifference to being deceived. In the public's view of the Iraq War, what mattered was whether it was succeeding, not whether it was being waged on false pretenses. The European public was much less tolerant of deception. Prime Minister Tony Blair of Great Britain was exposed to scathing criticism, and the Spanish public turned against José Maria Aznar when he tried to blame the terrorist attack in Madrid on the Basques.

The uncritical support for President Bush in the aftermath of 9/11 might be explained by the clever exploitation of that traumatic event by the administration. But that explanation does not go deep enough. The lack of concern with the truth predates 9/11. I attribute it to the adversarial character of the political and the judicial systems and the ever-sharper competition that prevails in all forms of economic and social activity. In 1996, when I decided to set up a domestic foundation, I identified as one of the shortcomings of American society an excessive admiration of success—measured in monetary terms—to the detriment of more intrinsic values. That is why I established programs to reinforce medicine and law as professions. Our legal system seeks to establish the truth by an adversarial process, but if the practitioners pursue success at all cost, the truth suffers. When a society admires success no matter how it is achieved, the safeguards against cheating and lying and other sharp practices are diminished. People become disillusioned and cease to expect high standards of integrity from their leaders. Being deceived does not come as a surprise.

The untrammeled pursuit of success provides an unstable basis for society. Stability requires a set of intrinsic values that are observed regardless of the consequences. This assertion can be supported by an appeal to economic theory: Only when the supply and demand curves are independently given do they determine an equilibrium price. When success is the only criterion, the way is wide open to initially self-reinforcing, but eventually self-defeating, boom-bust processes. I have explained how the process works in the financial markets. The same principle applies in other fields. Success breeds success until it fails to do so, and then the connection works in the opposite direction. That is what makes the uncritical pursuit of success inherently unstable.

Some of these difficulties were foreshadowed in my original model of open society. I spoke of instability and a deficiency of intrinsic values. But one important consideration I left out of account: Why should people care about the truth? The entire construct of open society is based on the assumption that the truth matters: The ultimate truth is beyond our reach, but the closer we get to reality, the better. I discussed the quest for certainty, but I took the quest for truth for granted.

Truth Versus Success

I must now question that assumption. In dealing with nature, the truth is paramount. We need to understand how the forces of nature work in order to exploit nature to our advantage. Knowledge of reality is a precondition of success. In human affairs, there is a shortcut to success. We can impose our will on other humans directly without going to the trouble of pursuing the truth. In these circumstances, we cannot take it for granted that the truth matters. Here is a weakness in the concept of open society that was not previously apparent. As I pointed out earlier, open society is based on an epistemological argument. If reality were independently given and not subject to human manipulation, then indeed the pursuit of truth would have to take precedence over self-delusion and the deception of others. Plato assigned the task to a philosopher king, and Popper argued that it is best achieved by a critical process because no philosopher is capable of attaining the ultimate truth. That is how he arrived at the concept of open society. But the underlying idea that reality is independent of what people think is inappropriate when reality has thinking participants. That is the point I was trying to make with the concept of reflexivity. Thinking is part of the reality we seek to understand. As a consequence, our understanding has to fall short of knowledge because we lack an independent criterion by which the truth of our statements can be judged. In these circumstances, why should we pursue an unattainable truth instead of manipulating the truth to our advantage? That is the question I failed to ask, and it took the reelection of President Bush to make me aware of it. For whatever reason, I am passionately committed to the quest for truth and I expected others to care about the truth as much as I do. But that was my personal bias, not a rational expectation.

Now that I have asked the question, I have a rational argument to show that the truth does matter. It is simply this: Reality can be manipulated by proclaiming certain self-serving statements to be truths, but the results are liable to diverge from expectations. To keep this divergence to a minimum, we must seek to understand reality, not just manipulate it. There is a reality beyond our will, and we must respect it if we want to succeed. So there is a connection between the pursuit of truth and the pursuit of success after all, but it is not as direct as it is in natural science.

I have to remind the reader that my argument is built on the correspondence theory of truth: A statement is true if, and only if, it corresponds to the facts. That means that I am using "truth" and "reality" interchangeably: When I say "respect for truth," I also mean "respect for reality." Truth means different things for different people. For Islamic fundamentalists, it means the Koran; for religious fundamentalists in the United States, it may mean creationism or intelligent design. So when I say that the truth matters, I extol the virtues of gaining a better understanding of reality. I hope this helps to clarify my argument.

This argument was recently put to the test by the Bush administration. It was guided by a belief—not expressly stated—that the truth can be manipulated. But look at the results: The invasion of Iraq has been a dismal failure, even when judged by the Bush administration's own objectives. This makes a strong case for the critical process that is at the heart of an open society.

Although it is relatively simple, the argument is a philosophical one, and the general public is not interested in philosophy; it is interested in results. This puts those who argue for the principles of open society at a tremendous disadvantage: They need a book, or at least a few paragraphs, to make their point, but those who want to manipulate the truth can do so with a catch-phrase such as the war on terror. The American public has shown itself remarkably susceptible to being manipulated. Why?

OPEN SOCIETY NOT UNDERSTOOD

The question has lead me to an interesting insight, which I touched upon in chapter one: America is an open society that does not understand the concept of open society and does not abide by its principles. The expression is often used by President Bush and others, but its implications are not properly understood.

The fact is that the concept of open society is not part of the American political tradition. American democracy is the product of the Enlightenment, and the Enlightenment put its faith in reason. Reality was seen as something separate and independent of reason, and it was reason's task to discover it. Since reason had an independent criterion at its disposal, perfect knowledge seemed attainable. For instance, the theory of perfect competition was based on the assumption of perfect knowledge.

The Enlightenment was a hopeful age. Reality was seen as virgin territory awaiting discovery, and knowledge was the tool that would give mankind command over that territory. The scope for reason seemed unlimited. It is only with the advance of knowledge that we discovered that reason has its limitations. Reflexivity is a relatively recent discovery—if it can be called that—and it is far from generally accepted.

American democracy is based on the division of powers, not on the recognition that the ultimate truth is beyond our reach. On the contrary, the preamble to the Declaration of Independence states: "We hold these truths to be self-evident." It goes on to describe the requirements of an open society in great detail, but their justification has nothing to do with imperfect understanding. There is a tension between the preamble and the rest of the text that gave rise to two schools of thought: the preamble to natural rights, the text to universal human rights. It is noteworthy that the doctrine of natural rights was elaborated by Leo Strauss, the concept of open society by Karl Popper. Strauss and Popper are contemporaries from Austria and Germany, respectively; both are scholars of Plato, but they passed each other like ships in the night. I did not find any reference to Leo Strauss in Popper's writings. Popper was my mentor, Leo Strauss was the mentor of Paul Wolfowitz, one of the architects of the invasion of Iraq.

Although the American public is not interested in abstract philosophical discussions, the fact that the concept of open society is not properly understood has had severe adverse consequences. Open society is built on the recognition that our understanding is imperfect and there is a reality beyond our will. The truth can be manipulated, but the extent to which the outcome will approximate our will depends on the extent to which our understanding approximates reality. This insight has been lacking in America. We have been pursuing success without much concern for the truth. As a result, we have become a feel-good society, unwilling to confront unpleasant realities. We want our elected leaders to make us feel good instead of telling us the truth. The outcome endangers not only our open society but also our dominant position in the world.

The danger to open society can be analyzed within my conceptual framework: the undue extension of executive power, the infringement of civil liberties at home and violation of human rights abroad, and the suspension of the critical process that rendered our policies counterproductive. The danger to our dominant position will take us beyond the framework because the framework is not designed to deal with questions of power.

Before we go beyond the framework, I must draw an important conclusion from the argument I have presented. For open society to exist and to survive, it is essential that people believe in open society as a desirable form of social organization. Not all the people—that would go against the grain of open society—but enough people with enough conviction to prevent them from straying too far from the principles of open society. Belief in open society is difficult to sustain because open society does not provide a fully fledged political program. It does so only in a closed society, in which people yearn for freedom. In an open society, the preservation of open society is necessary but not sufficient. People must decide what kind of open society they want to live in. That is why there are different political parties. But underlying the political debate there must be some agreement on the principles governing the critical process that is at the heart of an open society. Foremost among those principles is that the truth matters. Absent agreement on that principle the political contest deteriorates into a shameless manipulation of the truth. The Swift Boat Veterans for Truth, a group that denigrated John Kerry's Vietnam record with television advertising, provide a good example. The campaign was successful because people do not care about the truth. In a democracy, it is the electorate that has to keep the politicians and the political operatives honest. That is where America is failing. A feel-good society, far from being committed to the pursuit of truth, cannot face harsh realities. This leaves it vulnerable to all kinds of false ideologies, Orwellian newspeak, and other deceptions.

For America to remain an open society, people need to be committed to the pursuit of truth. This is not as easy as it was at the time of the Enlightenment because we have discovered reflexivity. Respect for the truth can no longer be taken for granted; it has become a matter of values. Intellectual honesty and integrity are the values that America needs to rediscover if it is to recover.

Many people blame the media for the current state of affairs. But the media merely serves the market. People want to be entertained, not informed, and that is the market the media seeks to serve. Most people receive their information about current affairs from television comedians. Of course, the media ought to do more than just cater to the market because journalism is supposed to be a profession. Free and pluralistic media are an essential institution of an open society, but most of the media has ceased to fulfill its institutional role. There are only a few remnants, too few to guarantee the critical process. When *The New York Times* allowed itself to be misled about whether Saddam Hussein possessed weapons of mass destruction, the public had no alternative source of information. The conservative propaganda machine has put tremendous pressure on the media, particularly television, not to produce inconvenient information and they have caved in, one by one. In the Iraq War, the media was embedded in the military forces. Add to this the concentration of media ownership and the emergence of a right-wing propaganda machine that pretends to be part of the media scene and it is clear that the media exacerbates the weaknesses of a feel-good society.

CHAPTER 4

A Feel-Good Society

Although it predates 9/11, America's turning into a feel-good society is a relatively recent development. The epithet definitely does not apply to the society that emerged from the Second World War. Harry Truman was not a feel-good president. He called it as he saw it, and he was considered typical of the small-town citizens who constituted the backbone of America. The Marshall Plan was an act of far-sighted statesmanship. It would have been more appropriate to describe America as a can-do society.

Somewhere between then and now a transformation took place. Ronald Reagan was definitely a feel-good president—and he has since been elevated to the ranks of the saints. His funeral was nothing short of canonization. What happened between 1950 and 1980? I am not very good at this kind of analysis, but I would attribute the transformation mainly to the rise of consumerism and the application of consumerism to politics. Since 1980, the unwillingness to face reality has been exacerbated by globalization. A global economy based on the principles of market fundamentalism is full of uncertainties from which many people are eager to escape.* Religious fundamentalism has also played an increasingly important role, although I am ill-qualified to analyze it. Fundamentalist religion seems to avoid the soul-searching that has characterized Christian religions since the time of Jesus and appears to do everything to reward the faithful by making them feel good.

How did consumerism come to dominate the economy? In the classical definition of economics formulated by my professor, Lionel Robbins, at the London School of Economics, economics was concerned with the allocation of scarce resources among unlimited needs.† The market dealt in commodities, the shape of the supply and demand curves was fixed and economic theory was concerned only with determining prices. Needless to say, the equilibrium price attained in a perfect market, where an infinite number of buyers and callers were competing with each other, assured the optimum allocation of resources. This remains the credo of market fundamentalists to this day. But perfect competition does not favor profits. It provides adequate compensation for the use of capital but nothing more. Entrepreneurs are motivated by profits. They have been busy inventing ever more sophisticated ways of generating profits. Inventions have, of course, been the driving force of economic progress. But in addition to product innovation, entrepreneurs have found other ways of enhancing their profits: differentiating their products from others, establishing monopolies, advertising, marketing. These activities destroyed the pristine purity of

*Erich Fromm, *Escape from Freedom* (New York: Holt, Rinehart and Winston, Inc.,1941).
†Lionel Robbins, *An Essay on the Nature and Significance of Economic Science* (London: Macmillan, 1932).

perfect competition. Supply and demand were no longer independently given because demand was artificially stimulated and markets no longer dealt in commodities but in brands. This tendency progressed inexorably because it was driven by the quest for profits. Firms no longer catered to needs but to desires and they manipulated and stimulated those desires. They employed ever more sophisticated methods of market research and motivational research. And the target of these methods, the consumer, did not remain unaffected. It responded to stimulation. That is how consumerism developed. It was fostered by corporations in their search for profits.*

Gradually, the methods developed for commercial purposes found a market in politics. This changed the character of politics. The original idea of elections was that candidates would come forward and announce what they stood for; the electorate would then decide whom they liked best. The supply of candidates and the preferences of the electorate were supposed to be independently given, just as in the theory of perfect competition. But the process was corrupted by the methods adopted from commercial life: focus groups and framing the messages. Politicians learned to cater to the desires of the electorate instead of propounding policies they believed in. The electorate did not remain unaffected. They chose the candidate who told them what they wanted to hear, but at the same time they could not avoid noticing that they were being manipulated; they were not surprised when their elected leaders deceived them. But there was no escape. The increasing sophistication of communication methods was built

*A four-part series on BBC Television, *The Century of the Self*, directed by Adam Curtis, produced by RDF Media for BBC Two, 2002.

into the system. That is how America became a feel-good society. It was fostered by politicians seeking to be elected.

Americans have plenty to feel good about. Democratic
capitalism as practiced in the United States has been highly
successful. Consumerism bolstered demand and the Great
Depression has become a distant memory. Prosperity has
bolstered consumerism, setting in motion a benign circle.
The United States emerged from the Second World War as
the dominant military and economic power. That power was
challenged by the Soviet Union, but eventually the West
won the Cold War. When the Soviet system collapsed, the
United States became the sole superpower. The United
States was also the main sponsor of globalization which, in
turn, has been a boon to the United States. But the dominant
position of the United States cannot be long maintained by
a feel-good society that is unwilling to confront unpleasant
realities.

THE WAR ON TERROR

On September 11, 2001, America was confronted by a
traumatic event that affected people individually and collec-
tively. Their personal sense of security was shattered, and
America's territorial integrity was violated to an even greater
degree than at Pearl Harbor. At Pearl Harbor, soldiers protecting the state were killed; at the World Trade Center,
civilians who were supposed to be protected by the state were
the victims. The Bush administration fostered and magnified
the fear that gripped the nation and used it to further its own
interests. The public lined up behind the president in the war

on terror and allowed him to engage in policies that would have been impossible in normal times.

But the war on terror was counterproductive. It embroiled the United States in an adventure that cannot succeed and from which it will be difficult to withdraw. In my judgment, it was in its response to 9/11 that the United States left reality behind and got lost in far-from-equilibrium territory. The terrorist attack was real indeed, and it required a strong response; but the response chosen by the Bush administration carried the nation into a fantasy land created by a misrepresentation of reality. What is worse, people still do not recognize the phantasmagoric element in the war on terror. I shall have a hard time getting my point across because the war on terror has been unquestioningly accepted by the public; indeed, it is seen as the natural response to the terrorist attacks of 9/11 even by those who are opposed to the Bush administration's policies.

In my interpretation, the war on terror is a false metaphor —the opposite of a fertile fallacy. It has been used by the Bush administration to further its own objectives, but those objectives are opposed to the principles of open society and harmful to the national interest. Eventually, the war on terror even proved detrimental to the Bush administration's own interests because it has had unintended adverse consequences: The invasion of Iraq turned into a disaster.

In reality, terrorists are best dealt with by methods other than waging war. War, by its very nature, claims innocent victims. When it is waged against terrorists who keep themselves hidden, the chances of creating innocent victims are even greater. We find terrorism abhorrent because it kills or maims innocent people to further a political cause. The war on terror evokes a similar response from those who are its victims as the terrorist attacks on 9/11 evoked in us. As a consequence, there are many more people willing to risk their lives to attack Americans today than there were on September 11, 2001.

The fact that waging war on terror sounds so obvious and natural makes it all the more dangerous. The expression has been finely honed. It started out as the war on terrorism, but "Terrorism" was chiseled down to "Terror." But the meaning is unclear: Does "terror" refer to our feelings or to an undefined and elusive enemy? Its vagueness allows the expression to cover more ground.

What makes the war on terror a false metaphor is that it is taken literally. Terror is an abstraction. One cannot wage war on an abstraction. We have the means to destroy any target as long as we can identify it, but terrorists rarely provide an identifiable target. When we declare war, we must find a target; but the target we choose is unlikely to be the right one. We have killed more innocent civilians in Iraq than the terrorists killed on 9/11. In addition to killing, we have also humiliated and tortured many Iraqis. By creating innocent victims, we have advanced the terrorists' cause. They can now depict *us* as the terrorists and enlist the support of their countrymen, just as President Bush has enlisted ours. We find this difficult to understand because we cannot envision ourselves as terrorists. Yet, that is exactly how we appear to many Iraqis.

The Bush administration and its imitators—many foreign governments have been eager to follow its lead—insist that a state cannot commit acts of terror. That contention must be challenged. It is best to start with terrorist acts committed by other states. On May 13, 2005, the troops of President Islam Karimov of Uzbekistan fired on demonstrators in Andijan, and they massacred several hundred unarmed civilians. I spoke with two journalists who were there. One of them had a bullet hole in her passport, which had been in the rucksack she carried on her back. That was an act of terrorism designed to cow the population into submission. Or take the destruction of Grozny by the Russian army; then ask what the difference is between Grozny in Chechnya and Falluja in Iraq. One hardly needs to mention the atrocities committed in Iraq at the prison of Abu Ghraib, which have been officially ascribed to a few aberrant soldiers.

In *The Bubble of American Supremacy*, I expounded the theory of victims turning into perpetrators, setting up a vicious circle of escalating violence. In my interpretation, the American public unwittingly turned perpetrator, but the Bush administration—perhaps not President Bush personally, but those who prevailed on him after 9/11—did so deliberately.

At the time of the terrorist attacks, the Bush administration was dominated by a group of ideologues who believed that the United States was not assertive enough in exploiting its military supremacy. They had already advocated the invasion of Iraq under the Clinton administration. They are generally referred to as the neoconservatives, or "neocons," but this label may be misleading because it is not clear whether Vice President Dick Cheney and Secretary of Defense Donald Rumsfeld who lead the group, qualify as neocons. In *The Bubble of American Supremacy*, I called the group the advocates of American supremacy. In the aftermath of 9/11, they prevailed on President Bush and used the war on terror as an excuse to invade Iraq.

It is now widely recognized that the invasion of Iraq was a mistake, perhaps the worst blunder in America's foreign policy, and it was perpetrated on false pretences. But the war on terror has remained the cornerstone of American policy, and no politician has dared attack it frontally—Democrats even less than Republicans. The way the war on terror has been conducted, however, has come under intense scrutiny. Torture, extraordinary rendition (an extra-judicial procedure by which terrorist suspects are sent to countries other than the United States for interrogation), and other questionable methods have been outlawed by Congress. Illegal wiretapping within the United States has raised a storm of protests. So I am hopeful that the metaphor is slowly eroding. I was critical of the war on terror from its inception, but I had to be careful about what I said for fear of antagonizing my audience. Now I may find my readers more receptive.

A state of war constitutes a threat to civil liberties. As commander in chief, the president enjoys extended executive powers. President Bush has used these powers to the full, engaging in illegal wiretapping, holding prisoners indefinitely, and treating them in contravention of the Geneva Conventions. His legal advisers have developed a juridical theory that seeks to justify unlimited executive power at a time of war. This has emboldened the President to assert, when he signed the McCain amendment prohibiting torture, that the law does not constrain his constitutional authority to disregard the law in certain undefined circumstances. This is just one example of this President's assertion of constitutional powers unchecked by Congress or the Courts. While unprecedented, there is a danger that it will be endorsed by a Supreme Court whose latest appointees come from the same school of thought.

The emerging juridical philosophy has far-reaching implications; It elevates the executive branch above the other two and it destroys the balance established by the division of powers. It abandons the universality of human rights in favor of double standards. It exempts certain spaces (i.e., Guantanamo), certain courts (i.e., military commissions), certain persons (i.e., enemy combatants), and certain practices (i.e., extraordinary rendition) from judicial review. This constitutional vision creates a growing gap between citizens and aliens and reduces the civil liberties of all citizens.*

The war on terror also threatens America's dominant role in the world. The leader of the world has many duties and objectives besides protecting itself from terror. By giving priority to the war on terror, it is neglecting its other obligations. The leader of the world cannot be concerned only with minimizing its own casualties; it must also avoid inflicting casualties on others. The way American troops have behaved in Iraq—first failing to stop the looting, then failing to protect the population, but shooting to protect themselves—has reinforced the insurgency and fed anti-American sentiment.

Since terrorists are invisible, they will never disappear. Since the war on terror is counterproductive, it is liable to generate more terrorists or insurgents than it can liquidate. As a result, we are facing a permanent state of war and the end of the United States as an open society. All men and women of good faith, regardless of party affiliation, must come together to reject the war on terror as a false and dangerous metaphor.

I want to make it clear that when I condemn the war on terror I am not denying the threat posed by al Qaeda and its offsprings. That threat is real and it requires a strong response. But the response must be directed at al Qaeda and its

*In the last two paragraphs, I have drawn heavily on Harold Koh's speech to the American Constitution Society.

offsprings and not at an abstraction. To make my argument more convincing, I ought to spell out the correct response, but that is not a simple matter. Reality is more complicated than a catchy slogan such as the war on terror. The response should have included intelligence gathering, precautionary measures, reassuring rather than scaring the American public, gaining the confidence and support of the Islamic public and, where appropriate, using military force. I need to emphasize this point in order to defend myself against the inevitable accusation that I want to ignore or appease the terrorists and leave America defenseless.

I supported the invasion of Afghanistan. That is where Osama bin Laden had his address and al Qaeda had its training camps. Afghanistan was a failed state that harbored terrorists; it was a legitimate target of attack. My contention was that military means should be used sparingly and civilian casualties kept to a minimum; waging war should be a last resort, not the primary method of fighting terrorism. If we had stuck to the invasion of Afghanistan and followed it up with a successful nation building exercise, we would be much farther along in reducing the terrorist threat than we are today.

In my previous book, I compared the course taken by the United States to a stock market bubble, and I identified 9/11 as the moment when we abandoned normalcy and entered far-from-equilibrium territory. We had become a feel-good society long before President George W. Bush was elected president, and the conservative movement that brought him to power had also originated much earlier; but until 9/11 these trends were kept within bounds by the checks and balances that normally keep our democracy stable. It is 9/11 that "changed everything," as President Bush likes to say.

How could that happen? As I see it, the terrorists touched a weak spot in the national psyche: the fear of death. The prospect of dying is the ultimate spoiler to feeling good. A feel-good society simply cannot accept death. Osama bin Laden correctly identified the one aspect in which militant Islam is superior to Western civilization: the fear of death. The perpetrators of 9/11 were not afraid to die.

The denial of death is a characteristic feature of our culture. I recognized it long before 9/11; that is why I set up the Project on Death as one of the first projects of my foundation in America. Little did I anticipate that the denial of death would have such far-reaching political consequences. The collapse of the twin towers of the World Trade Center was a traumatic event made personal for us all because we witnessed it on television. The Bush administration was eager to exploit that experience for its own purposes. This was the fateful combination that led the country astray. A fearful giant striking out wildly is a good definition of a bully. After the world had poured out its sympathy for America's agony, it came to see America as a bully. That is exactly what bin Laden had been hoping for.

When people are guided by fear, they abandon reason. They are capable of actions that violate their principles. The fear of death is a particularly strong emotion. The Bush Administration fostered this fear and appealed to the instinct of self preservation. But the appeal was unjustified. After all, the terrorist attack, tragic and traumatic as it was, did not really threaten the nation's existence. The Japanese attack on Pearl Harbor did more damage to our military might. After 9/11, the United States still remained the most powerful nation on earth. It could still project overwhelming military power to any part of the world.

The Bush administration declared the war on terror to further its own objectives. To this end, it magnified the danger instead of putting it in the proper perspective. The events of 9/11 were awesome in their own right, but the Bush administration suggested that terrorists might now gain possession of weapons of mass destruction. To quote President Bush: "America must not ignore the threat gathering against us. Facing clear evidence of peril, we cannot wait for the final proof—the smoking gun—that could come in the form of a mushroom cloud." Compare that with President Roosevelt's dictum: "The only thing we have to fear is fear itself."

Has there ever been a war with an unidentified enemy, undefined objectives, unknown rules, and an indefinite duration? Yet, by exploiting fear, that is what the Bush administration has induced the American public to accept as the natural and obvious response. So much so that when I say that we must renounce the war on terror as a false metaphor people simply do not understand what I am talking about.

I feel strongly that we cannot regain our balance until we repudiate the war on terror. Quietly adjusting our behavior will not do because our past behavior will continue to haunt us like a guilty secret. I have seen it happen in other countries. Greece refused to recognize Macedonia (it still carries the qualification "former Yugoslav Republic of Macedonia" in its name) because it had followed a policy of turning ethnic Macedonians into Greeks forty years previously. Turkey cannot admit to the Armenian massacres or to the mistreatment of Kurds. In the past, America, being an open society, has been more willing to recognize its past sins. The genocide of Native Americans has become part of the school curriculum, as has slavery. In the war on terror we have committed many shameful acts. We have sent our troops to suffer and die for an unjust cause. We have compromised the integrity and morale of our armed forces, lost the moral high ground and endangered our dominant position in the world. Who will enlighten the public?

We cannot count on the Democrats because they are afraid of being depicted as weak on defense. They will not be able to climb out of the box into which the Bush administration has put them without confronting the war on terror. They have to show that—contrary to what President Bush says—a military offense is not the best defense. But that is a high-risk strategy, and so far Democrats have been reluctant to adopt it. I see more hope on the Republican side. Senator John McCain has led the fight against torture and has prevailed. Other Republican congressmen are eager to dissociate themselves from the Bush administration. The White House has, to a large extent, lost control of Congress. There is life in our democratic institutions, after all.

In the years since 9/11, America's power and influence in the world have declined more than at any other time in its history. When the terrorists struck, the United States enjoyed unquestioned military superiority in the world. It could project its power to any part of the world, as the successful invasions of Afghanistan and Iraq have attested. America's domination of air, sea, and space remains unimpaired; but its ability to project power on land is constrained by the fact that its armed forces are overstretched and bogged down in Iraq. The really drastic shift, however, has occurred in political power and influence. In the aftermath of 9/11, we enjoyed almost universal sympathy and support in the world. Since then, public opinion has turned against us and almost every initiative that is backed by the United

States is greeted with suspicion and opposition by the rest of the world. Even a cursory look at the current state of affairs reveals that the decline in American power has been much greater than anybody could have anticipated. As a result, we are less secure and the world is less stable than it was when al Qaeda attacked the United States.

TURMOIL IN THE MIDDLE EAST

The United States has thoroughly destabilized the Middle East by invading Iraq. The task of the occupying forces is no longer confined to fighting a Sunni insurrection; they have to contain an incipient civil war. The country has divided along sectarian lines and each faction has established a fighting capacity. The Ministry of the Interior is in the hands of a radical Shiite Islamist party whose death squads maintain prisons and engage in extra-judicial executions. Some of the most reliable fighting units in the army consist of Kurdish Peshmerga. The level of fighting is contained by the presence of the United States but the primary objective of the occupying forces is to protect themselves, not the population. The civilian population can see the civil war coming and seeks safety by lining up with one side or the other. People relocate within the country or, if they can, abroad. Real estate prices in Amman, Jordan have gone through the roof. Those in mixed areas such as Baghdad, Kirkuk and Mosul are the most exposed and already suffer the most. At the time of writing (April 2006), the political process is in a stalemate and it is difficult to see a resolution in the absence of an overarching agreement with Iran. Even then, it is doubtful whether Iran can exercise sufficient influence over the Shiite factions. On the Sunni side, al Qaeda and other Salafist factions are hell-bent on provoking sectarian violence and the population is more afraid of the United States and Iraqi armies than of the terrorists. The situation is slowly but inexorably deteriorating and could widen into a regional Sunni-Shia conflict, especially if the United States reduces or withdraws its troops.

Iran has a vested interest in keeping Iraq friendly, weak, and somewhat unsettled, but it does not want a regional Shia-Sunni conflict or to have Iraq fall apart. After all, it was bogged down in a brutal war with Iraq for eight years and suffered immense casualties.

Iran is the major beneficiary of the invasion, which removed its enemy Saddam Hussein from power, tied up American forces in a task that they are ill-prepared to perform, and tightened the supply of oil. What a change from the situation that prevailed prior to 9/11! At that time, many Iranians were dissatisfied with the clerical regime. Mohammad Khatami was elected president in 1997 on a reform platform. Unfortunately, the hard-liners controlled the levers of power and he could not deliver on his promises. But the hard-liners remained beleaguered. The ground shifted after 9/11. President Bush named Iran a member of the "axis of evil," and Iranian public opinion rallied to the defense of the country. The invasions of Afghanistan and Iraq gave Iran greatly increased influence in these neighboring countries. Its nuclear program enjoyed widespread popular support. At the same time, the Bush administration's vocal advocacy for regime change made life difficult for the political opposition.

The Iranian elections in 2004 were skillfully stage-managed so that the opposition lost its voice in parliament and, in 2005, a rabid extremist was elected president. President Ahmadine-jad is not as strong internally as he may appear from the out-side because of incompetence. Three of his nominees for oil minister were rejected by a hard-liner parliament before he compromised and nominated a technocrat. This was a terri-ble humiliation for him and drove him to new extremes in anti-Zionist rhetoric. Oil production is eroding. Nevertheless, Iran is in the driver's seat. Even the fall in oil production plays to its hand by tightening global supplies. But these conditions may not last and Iran has decided to exploit them by accelerating its nuclear program. This is a direct reflection of American weakness, and it poses a greater threat to the world than the one Saddam Hussein was supposed to have represented. If Iran develops a nuclear capability, it will become a regional su-perpower; as a result, the Gulf region will be threatened and the very existence of Israel will be in peril. No countermea-sures are likely to deter Iran from its course because the regime finds itself in a win-win situation. Either it gets the bomb or it gets bombed; either way, the regime benefits. A missile attack on Iran would heighten anti-American senti-ment, consolidate popular support for the regime, and do un-told damage to the world economy. The position of the occupying forces in Iraq may well become untenable.

The United States has succeeded in passing a UN Security Council declaration, not resolution, that admonishes Iran to suspend its uranium enrichment activities and to allow the In-ternational Atomic Energy Agency to monitor its compliance with the declaration. That is the most that Russia and China are willing to tolerate, but it may be sufficient to provide a ve-neer of legitimacy for a missile attack. We are set on a collision course, and the only question is how much time is left. There is every reason to delay the decision as long as possible because neither alternative—Iran as a nuclear power or a missile attack against Iran—is palatable and conditions may improve with the passage of time. The time could be used to develop a new approach to nuclear nonproliferation that would strengthen the hand of the international community in dealing with Iran. Unfortunately, time is short, because Russia has sold Iran Tor and S300 missiles that will render an attack less feasible, after they are installed in the fall of 2006. I shall discuss the subject in greater detail in the next chapter. I believe there is a possibility of finding an accommodation with Iran and that is our best hope for avoiding a conflict that could have even more disastrous consequences than the invasion of Iraq, but that would require a more thorough reorientation of America's posture than this administration is capable of.

Islam, like any great religion, contains a variety of traditions and attitudes. Under the influence of terrorism and the American response, the militant tradition is on the ascendant almost everywhere, including both Sunni and Shia, Islam's two major sects. This is apparent in recent election results. Under American pressure, Egypt has held multiparty elections in which the Sunni Moslem Brotherhood was not allowed to participate; nevertheless, many of its supporters were elected in their individual capacity. The Syrian-and Iranian-supported militant organization, Hezbollah, did well in Lebanon, where it garnered most of the Shia votes. In Palestine, Hamas, a Sunni militant organization closely associated with the Moslem Brotherhood, emerged victorious and formed the government. Both Hamas and Hezbollah have been declared terrorist organizations by the United States but Arabs hold a different opinion.

In Iraq, Shiite Islamist parties backed by Iran won two popular elections and now dominate the government. Their victory invigorated a Sunni-based insurgency that has become increasingly extreme. One group of insurgents comprises jihadi Salafis, who engage in terrorism against Shiite civilians. The rise of both radical Shiism and Salafism is a dramatic departure from Saddam's Baathist regime.* It means Islamist radicalism has become the dominant political force in what had been one of the most secular Arab countries.

In these circumstances, the Bush administration's insistence on holding free elections can be destabilizing for America's allies. Democratizing the Middle East became a top priority of the Bush administration after the other arguments for invading Iraq proved to be unsustainable but the policy is incompatible with the war on terror and the need for Middle Eastern oil. The elections in Egypt were hardly free, nevertheless the results made the regime very nervous. After the recent elections, the main nonreligious opposition leader was put into jail on trumped-up charges and the promised local elections were postponed for two years. The victory of Hamas in Palestine has thrown the international community into disarray. Saudi Arabia is proceeding very cautiously. President Pervez Musharraf of Pakistan simply resists the American pressure and the administration acquiesces because of Musharraf's precarious position. I am afraid the incompatibility between democratization and the war on terror will result in the Bush administration quietly abandoning its policy of democratization. As I shall argue in the next chapter, that would be the wrong choice.

*International Crisis Group, "The Next Iraqi War? Sectarianism and Civil Conflict," pp. 14–22, at http://www.crisisgroup.org.

Something is fundamentally wrong with President Bush's contention that he has made us safer at home by taking the war on terror abroad. There are many more people willing to sacrifice their lives to kill Americans than there were on 9/11. Abu Musab al-Zarqawi has established a strong enough base in Iraq that he can export terrorism abroad—to Jordan so far. Militant Islam is gaining ground in other countries and moderate pro-Western Arab regimes are beleaguered. They are caught between the pressure to democratize and the increasingly militant Islamism of their populations. At the same time, they are discriminated against in the United States, as the popular resistance to Dubai's thwarted attempt to buy port operations from another foreign entity, P&O Ports North America, demonstrated. The Bush administration's rhetoric on the terrorist threat backfired by making the American public suspicious of all Arabs. The Arab elite, which used to be educated in the United States now feels more comfortable elsewhere.

The Bush administration shows no awareness of the contradictions in its policies or of the negative consequences. I attach President Bush's introduction to the 2006 National Security Strategy so that readers can judge for themselves. It contains some modifications and changes of emphasis from the unilateralist tone of the 2002 document, but on the whole it is a reaffirmation of failed policies. The underlines are mine.

The situation in the Middle East is dire. Iran threatens to become a nuclear power. The low-grade civil war in Iraq threatens to broaden into a regional conflict. We are facing a clash of civilizations and/or armed sectarian conflict. And all this in a region that is responsible for the bulk of the world's oil supply.

THE WHITE HOUSE

WASHINGTON

My fellow Americans,

America is at war. This is a wartime national security strategy required by the grave challenge we face – the rise of terrorism fueled by an aggressive ideology of hatred and murder, fully revealed to the American people on September 11, 2001. This strategy reflects our most solemn obligation: to protect the security of the American people.

America also has an unprecedented opportunity to lay the foundations for future peace. The ideals that have inspired our history – freedom, democracy, and human dignity – are increasingly inspiring individuals and nations throughout the world. And because free nations tend toward peace, the advance of liberty will make America more secure.

These inseparable priorities – fighting and winning the war on terror and promoting freedom as the alternative to tyranny and despair – have now guided American policy for more than 4 years.

We have kept on the offensive against terrorist networks, leaving our enemy weakened, but not yet defeated.

We have joined with the Afghan people to bring down the Taliban regime – the protectors of the al-Qaida network – and aided a new, democratic government to rise in its place.

We have focused the attention of the world on the proliferation of dangerous weapons – although great challenges in this area remain.

We have stood for the spread of democracy in the broader Middle East – meeting challenges yet seeing progress few would have predicted or expected.

We have cultivated stable and cooperative relations with all the major powers of the world.

We have dramatically expanded our efforts to encourage economic development and the hope it brings – and focused these efforts on the promotion of reform and achievement of results.

We led an international coalition to topple the dictator of Iraq, who had brutalized his own people, terrorized his region, defied the international community, and sought and used weapons of mass destruction.

And we are fighting alongside Iraqis to secure a united, stable, and democratic Iraq – a new ally in the war on terror in the heart of the Middle East.

We have seen great accomplishments, confronted new challenges, and refined our approach as conditions changed. We have also found that the defense of freedom brings us loss and sorrow, because freedom has determined enemies. We have always known that the war on terror would require great sacrifice – and in this war, we have said farewell to some very good men and women. The terrorists have used dramatic acts of murder – from the streets of Fallujah to the subways of London – in an attempt to undermine our will. The struggle against this enemy – an enemy that targets the innocent without conscience or hesitation – has been difficult. And our work is far from over.

America now faces a choice between the path of fear and the path of confidence. The path of fear – isolationism and protectionism, retreat and retrenchment – appeals to those who find our challenges too great and fail to see our opportunities. Yet history teaches that every time American leaders have taken this path, the challenges have only increased and the missed opportunities have left future generations less secure.

This Administration has chosen the path of confidence. We choose leadership over isolationism, and the pursuit of free and fair trade and open markets over protectionism. We choose to deal with challenges now rather than leaving them for future generations. We fight our enemies abroad instead of waiting for them to arrive in our country. We seek to shape the world, not merely be shaped by it; to influence events for the better instead of being at their mercy.

The path we have chosen is consistent with the great tradition of American foreign policy. Like the policies of Harry Truman and Ronald Reagan, our approach is idealistic about our national goals, and realistic about the means to achieve them.

To follow this path, we must maintain and expand our national strength so we can deal with threats and challenges before they can damage our people or our interests. We must maintain a military without peer – yet our strength is not founded on force of arms alone. It also rests on economic prosperity and a vibrant democracy. And it rests on strong alliances, friendships, and international institutions, which enable us to promote freedom, prosperity, and peace in common purpose with others.

Our national security strategy is founded upon two pillars:

The first pillar is promoting freedom, justice, and human dignity – working to end tyranny, to promote effective democracies, and to extend prosperity through free and fair trade and wise development policies. Free governments are accountable to their people, govern their territory effectively, and pursue economic and political policies that benefit their citizens. Free governments do not oppress their people or attack other free nations. Peace and international stability are most reliably built on a foundation of freedom.

The second pillar of our strategy is confronting the challenges of our time by leading a growing community of democracies. Many of the problems we face – from the threat of pandemic disease, to proliferation of weapons of mass destruction, to terrorism, to human trafficking, to natural disasters – reach across borders. Effective multinational efforts are essential to solve these problems. Yet history has shown that only when we do our part will others do theirs. America must continue to lead.

GEORGE W. BUSH
THE WHITE HOUSE
March 16, 2006

An Unstable World Order

American power and influence is also waning outside the Middle East. China and Russia have seen their regional influence grow. China's hand has been strengthened vis-à-vis the United States because America depends on China to act as an intermediary with North Korea. China is helpful but only up to a point because it benefits from the continuation of the conflict. The British used to call it providing all aid short of help. In my opinion, China is gaining political power and influence far too fast for its own good. At the same time, the leadership has been made extremely nervous by the so-called color revolutions in Georgia and Ukraine. The net result has been a reversal in political liberalization.

The Putin regime in Russia has also suffered a severe setback from the color revolutions. Putin's popularity had rested, to a large extent, on the unspoken promise that he would reconstitute the Russian empire. The color revolutions deflated these aspirations. Putin responded by becoming increasingly authoritarian; he asserted his power not only over the government but also over the courts, the media, the political opposition and civil society. But Russia is just too large to be governed from the Kremlin. The regime committed a number of administrative blunders and the economy is not benefiting sufficiently from the high price of oil. Putin is using Russian control over gas supplies to enrich his associates and allies and to reassert Russia's influence on its neighbors. President Bush hailed the color revolutions as victories for freedom, but he is not in a position to arrest Russia's authoritarian tendencies. Putin's hand has been strengthened by the tight energy supply situation.

The Shanghai Cooperation Organization established in 2001 has brought China and Russia together with the Central Asian republics. One of the main objectives is to reduce American influence in the region. After the color revolutions, Putin and the authoritarian rulers in Central Asia agreed among themselves to support each other in repressing social unrest. This led to a massacre in Andijan, when the president of Uzbekistan, Islam Karimov, wanted to signal that the government would not tolerate public protests challenging its authority. Subsequently, he was feted in Beijing and supported by Russia. The United States was forced to close its airbase in Uzbekistan.

There is also increasing cooperation between China, Russia, and Iran, particularly in energy matters, but it is premature to speak of a countervailing block because China cannot afford to alienate the United States to that extent, although Russia has become increasingly assertive, selling a missile defense system to Iran. It is more accurate to say that President Bush has promoted nationalism and the rest of the world is following his lead. Nationalism prevails almost everywhere. Tensions have risen between China and Japan, and Japan is lining up with the United States. The trouble is that Japanese nationalism is raising hackles in the rest of Asia; the United States, therefore, may find itself on the wrong side. China has been pushing for an alliance of the Association of Southeast Asian Nations (ASEAN) with China, Japan, and Korea (ASEAN + 3). The ASEAN countries, fearing Chinese domination, have insisted on including India and Australia (ASEAN + 5). The appeal of both formations is that it excludes the United States.

The invasion of Iraq has contributed to tightening oil supplies. Countries hostile to the United States, such as Iran and Venezuela, have seen their bargaining position improve. China and India are increasingly nervous abut securing access to oil reserves. The United States made the mistake of not allowing a Chinese oil company to acquire the American firm Unocal, and this has further encouraged China to deal with rogue regimes. The correct policy would have been to allow the transaction to go forward on the condition that China cooperated with the international community in putting pressure on rogue regimes such as Myanmar. As it is, China has become the protector of Myanmar. China is also increasingly influential in Africa and South America.

Venezuela has emerged as a hostile power in South America. Benefiting from the high price of oil and anti-American sentiment, Hugo Chavez has been able to consolidate his position at home and extend his influence abroad. He has bought the allegiance of the Caribbean countries by supplying cheap oil and gained an ally in Bolivia, where Evo Morales, leader of the coca growers' association, was elected president on an anti-American and anti-globalization platform with an overwhelming majority. Dissatisfaction with the slow pace of economic progress and disillusionment with democracy is on the rise throughout the continent, with the notable exception of Chile, and American influence is at a low ebb.

America's weakness has also had a deleterious effect on its main ally, the European Union. American influence, epitomized by Donald Rumsfeld's talk about "old Europe," has been divisive, and nationalist sentiments have also risen. The new European Union Constitution was rejected in France and the Netherlands and the European Union is in crisis. But the problems of Europe cannot be blamed on the Bush administration; they deserve to be considered separately. Europe is an open society and its crisis is contemporaneous with, but distinct from, the crisis of open society in America.

This is not meant to be a comprehensive geopolitical survey of the world. The selection of facts is deliberately biased against the Bush administration. I did not mention, for instance, the conversion of Muammar Khadaffi in Libya, improved relations with India, or John Howard becoming an imitation of George W. Bush in Australia. But enough facts have been cited to ensure that no listing of facts on the opposite side could possibly counterbalance the contention that America's position has declined precipitously since 9/11. Add the rising domestic opposition to the Iraq War, and it is clear that if it continues on its present course America is liable to loose its dominant position in the world sooner than seemed possible when the Bush doctrine was promulgated. This would be a loss not just for America but for the world. In spite of the blemishes on its record, the United States has been a stabilizing influence in the world and its decline has created instability.

The Concept of Power

The deterioration in America's position can be attributed almost entirely to a fundamental misconception about the nature of power that guided the Bush administration, at least in its first term. There have been some attempts to correct course in the second term, but they have not made much headway because the legacy of the first term has done too much damage. Take the issue of torture and extraordinary rendition: Most of the incidents occurred during the first term, but they poisoned relations with Europe in the second term because the Bush administration was unwilling to admit and renounce its own practices. The group led by Dick Cheney and Donald Rumsfeld that is responsible for those practices is still part of the Bush administration.

The Cheney clique of American supremacists believe that international relations are relations of power, not law. In their view, international law merely ratifies what power has wrought, and they define power in terms of military might. These ideas are misconceived. Power is a tricky word; it belongs in the realm of natural science, where it can be precisely defined and measured. When the word "power" is applied to human affairs, it is used metaphorically and its various facets cannot be reduced to a common denominator. A Nobel Prizewinning scientist can be knocked down by an illiterate thug; a powerful dictator can be exploited by a quack or turn into putty in the hands of his wife or mistress. Power is rather like the children's game called "scissors, paper, stone": Scissors can cut the paper, paper can cover the stone, and stone can crush the scissors.

Comparing power to a children's game sounds like a joke, but it provides an insight into the limitations of power that has escaped the attention of our leaders. When someone has absolute supremacy and abuses it, some other way may be found to puncture that supremacy. Without excusing it, terrorism can be interpreted as a response to military supremacy: The paper that covers the stone.

The advocates of American supremacy have turned power into a false metaphor—not unlike that other false metaphor, the war on terror. Indeed, the two false metaphors are different facets of the same distorted worldview. It may come as a surprise how much damage false metaphors can do, but it is difficult to find another explanation for the precipitous decline in American power and influence. After all, what Marxists would call the material conditions—military, economic, and financial strengths—could not change all that much in five years. It is the ideological superstructure that has done all the damage. This gives ground for hope—false ideas can be corrected more easily than material conditions. Unfortunately, it takes time for a distorted interpretation of reality to make its effect felt. What is worse, a false metaphor can be effective in serving a hidden purpose—for instance, the war on terror has enabled President Bush to gain popularity at home. In other words, false metaphors tend to be initially self-reinforcing; but later, when their falsehood is revealed for all to see, they will become self-defeating. We are now at that stage.

MATERIAL CONDITIONS

There has also been some deterioration in the material conditions of the United States since 2001, but it is a gradual process and constitutes less of a discontinuity than the conduct of policy. As discussed, The United States still enjoys unquestioned military superiority. While it can no longer project its power to any part of the world, the United States is still in control of the air, the seas, and space. It will not soon engage in another ground war but it can still hit targets with missiles.

On the economic front, the trade deficit continues to rise. It had reached 6.2 percent of GDP (gross domestic product) by the fourth quarter of 2005, but that is a trend that started well before George W. Bush became president. The budget deficit amounts to 2.6 of our GDP. This contrasts with the significant surplus that the country enjoyed at the end of the Clinton administration. Both deficits can be attributed to consumerism and our feel-good society. George W. Bush catered to the feel-good factor by using Clinton's legacy of a budget surplus for a massive tax cut. He failed to pay for either the war on terror or the war in Iraq.

American consumerism, coupled with Asian mercantilism, has kept the world economy going. Whenever there was a financial crisis, or other setback, in the world economy, the United States financial authorities injected another dose of monetary stimulus; U.S. lending institutions then eased credit conditions another notch. The Asian financial authorities are happy to finance the resulting United States trade deficit by buying U.S. bonds and bills. There is a symbiotic relationship between the American desire to consume and the Asian propensity to save that could keep the trade imbalance growing indefinitely. Nevertheless, I believe the music is about to stop—not because of the trade imbalance but because of the inability of the American consumer to borrow more. Credit has been stretched to the limit. Cars can be bought on five-year credit with no money down. Houses can be bought with interest-only mortgages and practically no equity investment. Lending institutions are willing to lend with no questions asked and they offer below-market interest rates, so called teaser-rates, for up to eighteen months. It is difficult to see how credit conditions can be relaxed any further.*

*I have since learned that car financing can extend to eighty-four months. This renders car owners' equity always negative.

Under the stimulus of low-interest rates and easy credit conditions, a housing boom developed that took on the character of a bubble. With house prices rising at double digits and interest rates in single digits, many houses were bought and held as speculation. At the same time, the rise in house prices has fuelled consumption. People refinanced their houses and withdrew the equity. Equity withdrawal reached an annual rate of over $800 billion in 2005, which is more than the trade deficit. It is estimated that about half that amount was actually spent. The household savings rate has fallen to negative 0.5 percent at the time of this writing (April 2006). This is well below the historical norm. It cannot last.

The tide is about to turn. The Federal Reserve has raised the fed funds rate from 1 percent to close to 5 percent; it has also issued a directive tightening the conditions under which lending institutions can finance house purchases. The rise in house prices has already started to abate. It remains to be seen whether the authorities can engineer a "soft landing." In my opinion, we are going to experience what will appear to be a soft landing, but it is likely to continue until it turns into a hard one. I cannot see how the double-digit rise in house prices can be rekindled because the overhang of excess supply has to be worked off. When the wealth effect of the housing bubble wears off, households will increase their savings and consume less. I expect that the U.S. economy will slow down in 2007, and the slowdown will be transmitted to the rest of the world via a weaker dollar. Neither the public nor the authorities seem to be properly prepared.

There is another major cause for concern: The energy supply situation. The problem has many facets: America's dependence on imported oil, global warming, political vulnerabilities. The Bush administration has been in denial on all fronts. In his latest State of the Union message, President Bush has spoken disapprovingly of America's addiction to oil, but his policies belie his words.

How can the public be convinced that under this administration the country has embarked on a disastrous course? The message is simple: America cannot remain powerful and prosperous as a feel-good society. We must learn to confront unpleasant realities if we want to remain leaders in the world. Will any politician stand up and deliver the message? And if there is such a politician, will the public listen? After all, a feel-good society does not want to be given bad news. As I said earlier, it is not enough to change governments; our attitudes and policies need to be thoroughly reconsidered.

CHAPTER 5

What's Wrong
with the World Order?

In the last chapter, I explored the implications of the Bush administration's policies, particularly the war on terror, on the United States. But that is only part of my concern. I was born in Hungary, persecuted as a Jew, moved to London before emigrating to New York, became committed to the universal idea of open society, traded in the global financial markets, and established foundations first in the former Soviet empire and then in the rest of the world: My main concern is with the world order and the future of mankind.

The United States is the dominant power in the world today. It sets the agenda to which the rest of the world has to respond. President Bush has set the wrong agenda. His administration was guided by the belief that international relations are relations of power, not law; since the United States is the sole superpower, it is entitled to impose its will on the world. This misconception has had disastrous consequences not only for America but also for the rest of the world.

The world order is based on the sovereignty of states. Sovereignty is an anachronistic concept born of an era when society consisted of rulers and subjects, not citizens. Sovereignty became the cornerstone of international relations with the Treaty of Westphalia in 1648. After thirty years of religious wars, it was agreed that the ruler had the right to determine the religion of his subjects: *Cuius regio eius religio.* The French Revolution overthrew King Louis XVI and the people seized sovereignty. In principle, sovereignty has belonged to the people ever since.

There have always been rules governing the relationship between states, but these rules could always be broken by the use of superior force. There has never been a world order capable of preventing war, although some arrangements have been more satisfactory than others. Nevertheless, the idea that there is no world order other than the use of force is a fallacy—a companion piece to the misinterpretation of the nature of power. The idea appealed to the advocates of American supremacy because it would have allowed the United States to impose its will on the world. But it did not work. When the terrorist attacks of September 11, 2001, gave the Bush administration the opportunity to translate the idea into practice, the outcome was far removed from expectations. The ideology of American supremacy found expression in the Bush doctrine incorporated in the National Security Report of 2002. Its two main tenets held that the United States must maintain absolute military superiority in every part of the world and that the United States has the right to preemptive military action. At the time the doctrine was promulgated, the United States was, in fact, in a position to project overwhelming force in any part of the world.* But, as I mentioned earlier, by engaging in preemptive war in Iraq, the United States lost that position. Judging by the Bush administration's own objectives, the invasion of Iraq was a colossal blunder.

The world cannot be ruled by military force. Military power is only one of many ingredients that a country needs to exercise influence over others. Imperial powers did not succeed by the force of arms alone. Even the Ottoman Empire, which was built by conquest, had an elaborate system for maintaining peace and justice and the empire disintegrated when the system broke down.

The United States did not become the dominant power by military means. Victory in the Second World War was followed by the establishment of the United Nations and the Bretton Woods institutions (the International Monetary Fund and the World Bank) and the Marshall Plan. The behavior of the United States was not always exemplary—the CIA was busy hatching plots, planning assassinations, and arranging coups d'état; but most of these activities were clandestine, and when they were revealed, the CIA was reined in. The Vietnam War ended in defeat and broke the can-do spirit that had characterized America until then. (Lyndon Johnson had put forward his Great Society project before he renounced his candidacy for reelection on account of the Vietnam War). The United States continued to fight proxy wars and to sustain authoritarian regimes. Remember the Iran-Contra affair? But these were aberrations. On the whole, the United States ful-

---

*That was true with regard to North Korea as well. What made military action impractical is that the capital of South Korea, Seoul, is within artillery range of North Korea and millions of South Koreans would be killed *before* the United States could destroy North Korea's military power.

filled its role as leader of the free world reasonably well. The rest of the free world willingly accepted American leadership against the Communist threat, and the United States was supportive of its allies. For instance, it played a constructive role in the evolution of the European Union and fostered the economic development of Japan and the other East Asian Tigers. The United States could be a superpower and the leader of the free world at the same time. The Communist threat served as a force for cohesion in a society characterized by the pursuit of individual self-interest and self-satisfaction.

This comfortable identity was disrupted by the collapse of the Soviet empire. Being the sole superpower and the leader of the free world was no longer the same thing, but the United States failed to recognize it. America used its dominant position to promote its national self-interest in every sphere, economic as well as military. That is not what the leader of the world is supposed to do. In a world order consisting of sovereign states, the United States, as the dominant power, has to concern itself with the well-being of humanity in addition to pursuing its self-interest. This unique responsibility derives from the privileged position that the United States occupies in the world. It is in charge of the agenda. It cannot unilaterally impose its will on the world, but no collective, cooperative action is possible without its leadership or active cooperation. The United States can block every international institution. It has veto power in the United Nations Security Council and it is the only country that has a blocking minority in the Bretton Woods institutions. Washington determines the direction in which the world will move, but the rest of the world does not have a vote in Congress; therefore it falls to the leadership in Washington to give due weight to the common interests of humanity in addition to the national interests of the United States.

When the United States first became the world's dominant power, it acknowledged this unique responsibility. A genuine concern for the future of humanity infused President Franklin Roosevelt's words and actions. After the Second World War, the United States was magnanimous with its defeated enemies and envisioned a better world order in which the horrors of the war could not be repeated. President Roosevelt's vision was not realized, but it inspired respect. America was too successful and prosperous to be loved, but it was able to maintain its dominant position partly because it was so admired and imitated. There has been a profound shift in American attitudes since the Marshall Plan was implemented. When the Soviet Union collapsed, the idea of a Marshall Plan for the former Soviet empire could not even be discussed. In 1988, I raised the subject at an international conference in Potsdam, then still part of East Germany, and I was literally laughed at. I raised it again with Robert Zoellick, who was a key advisor to George H. W. Bush, and he told me that Mikhail Gorbachev must first break with Fidel Castro. By the time Russia had fulfilled all the demands made upon it, it was in a state of total collapse and deemed beyond repair. At a Thomas Jefferson anniversary dinner in 1993, I tried to convince President Clinton that Russia was going through a process similar to the one the United States had faced in Jefferson's time, and that Russia needed and deserved our support; but to no avail. President Clinton stressed competitiveness, not generosity.

The emergence of a different attitude from the one that gave birth to the Marshall Plan can be identified with the

election of Ronald Reagan. I have called it "market fundamentalism"—a belief that the common interest is best served
by people pursuing their self-interest. According to this view,
the unique responsibility I am talking about does not make
any sense: There is no need for the strong to look after the
weak. This belief is based on a misinterpretation of the market mechanism. Markets are supposed to tend towards an
equilibrium that assures the optimum allocation of resources.
But that is not how markets, particularly financial markets,
work. They do not tend towards equilibrium and they are not
designed to ensure social justice. Unobstructed markets are
very efficient in allocating resources among competing private needs, or, since the spread of consumerism, desires. But
there are collective needs, such as maintaining peace and order, protecting the environment, and preserving the market
mechanism itself, that are not taken care of by market forces.
Collective needs can be turned into market forces by creating
the right incentives and penalties, but this requires political
action. Indeed, translating collective needs into market forces is
often the best way to take care of them, but ignoring them altogether brings some unfortunate consequences. Not only
does ignoring collective needs favor the rich at the expense of
the poor—an outcome that market fundamentalists welcome,
but it also leaves some issues like global warming completely
unattended—and that cannot be good for the rich, either.

The rise of globalization, which I date to the influence of
Ronald Reagan in the United States and Margaret Thatcher
in the United Kingdom in the early 1980s, has been a market
fundamentalist project. Facilitating the international movement of capital has made it difficult for individual countries to
tax or regulate capital. Since capital is an essential factor of

production, governments have to pay more attention to the requirements of international capital than to their own citizens.

The current form of globalization has resulted in a lopsided world order: The development of international institutions has not kept pace with the growth of global financial markets. Private capital movements far outweigh the facilities of the International Monetary Fund and the World Bank. Developing countries are vying to attract capital, yet the world's savings are being sucked up to finance overconsumption in the United States.

I used to inveigh against the inequities of globalization but my attention shifted when the advocates of American supremacy gained the upper hand in the Bush administration. It is one thing when the survival of the fittest is pursued in the economic sphere and quite another when it finds expression in military action. That is what led me to invoke the boom-bust analogy. In response to the terrorist attacks of 9/11, the Bush administration embarked on a course that was initially self-reinforcing, but eventually it was bound to turn self-defeating. The turn came too late to prevent the reelection of President Bush, but it came just the same. It took the war on terror and the invasion of Iraq to turn our erstwhile allies against us. Now that the American public has also turned against the Iraq War, the Bush administration is in full retreat.

Here, my primary concern is to drive home the full implications of the misconceptions that have guided our policies since 9/11. Not only has American power and influence suffered a serious setback, but the world order is in disarray. In a world of sovereign states, the lack of a dominant power that has the common interests of humanity at heart leads to instability and conflict. Humanity has acquired tremendous control over the forces of nature. That control can be used both for constructive and destructive purposes. It is not an exaggeration to say that our civilization could be destroyed by armed conflict, or even by the neglect of common interests, such as combating global warming. That is why it is so important to correct our misconceptions.

It is not enough to reestablish the status quo that prevailed prior to 9/11; we have to rethink America's role in the world more profoundly. It was only after 9/11 that America entered far-from-equilibrium territory; but the seeds of that deviation were sown much earlier when market fundamentalism emerged as the dominant ideology and American leadership gave globalization the shape it took. This goes back to Ronald Reagan's presidency. The world order needs a major overhaul. Much more is at stake than regaining the privileged position the United States used to occupy. I do not want to sound bombastic, but I genuinely believe that our civilization is at stake.

No overhaul is possible without the leadership, or at least the participation, of the United States. That is why we need to engage in a profound rethinking of our role in the world. It is not enough to disentangle ourselves from Iraq; we must also repudiate the war on terror. It is not enough to revert to the foreign policy we used to conduct before 9/11; we must acknowledge and live up to our unique responsibility as leaders of the free world. An open society ought to be able to learn from its mistakes—and find a more effective way to deal with terrorism.

I am not advocating a radically new world order, only a change of attitude; from the single-minded pursuit of national self-interest to showing some concern for the common interests of humanity. Even that idea may be utopian.

Again, I wish to emphasize that a feel-good society does not like to face unpleasant truths. Our politicians are unwilling to question the war on terror; will they tell the electorate about our unique responsibility for the world? How will that stack up against the interests of their constituencies? I am afraid that the United States may have to suffer further reverses before Americans will be willing to rededicate themselves to the principles of open society. By the time that happens, the United States may no longer be the dominant power it used to be.

I shall take the prevailing world order as my starting point and consider how it could be improved. A comprehensive review is beyond the scope of this book. I shall focus on a few issues that I consider the most pressing unsolved problems: How can we foster democracy and deal with the likes of Saddam Hussein? How can we address nuclear proliferation and global warming? How can we deal with the resource curse? How can we keep the global economy on an even keel and reduce its iniquities? As I mentioned before, the selection of these problem areas already reflects my bias. I shall consider each of them in turn.

FOSTERING DEMOCRACY

The Bush Approach

In his second inaugural address, President Bush made the promotion of democracy throughout the world the centerpiece of his program. As the reader knows, I have a network of foundations dedicated to fostering open societies, and for this reason I ought to have welcomed his newfound interest. At first I was tempted to do so, but I soon discovered that his efforts, like so many others, are liable to prove counterproductive because they are based on false pretenses and a false interpretation of reality. Just as the invasion of Iraq has made it more difficult to deal with the likes of Saddam Hussein, President Bush's rhetoric will stand in the way of genuine efforts to foster democratic development. For instance, calling for regime change in Iran has hurt the advocates of open society there.

Democracy cannot be introduced by force of arms. Germany and Japan became democracies after the Second World War, but that war was not fought to introduce democracy. Germany and Japan were the aggressors, and when they lost the war they were ready for a change of heart. The generous treatment they received at the hands of the victors reinforced their willingness to adopt a new political system. That is not the case in Iraq.

The Approach of My Foundations

Introducing democracy from the outside is a tricky business because the prevailing world order is based on the sovereignty of states, and states are entitled to resist outside intervention. My foundations do not hesitate to get involved in the internal affairs of countries—after all, democracy is an internal affair—but they do it as citizens of the country concerned. The network consists of local foundations whose board and staff are preponderantly local citizens and they take responsibility for the actions of the foundations.

Each foundation has followed its own path—some more successfully than others—but there are some common features. We pursue a two-track strategy: supporting civil society and helping the government become more democratic and more effective. Open society is often confused with civil society, but it also needs a functioning government with which civil society can interact. If we engage in capacity building it is in cooperation with the government—no violation of sovereignty is involved. Where the government is receptive, the foundation can accomplish more; where it is hostile, the foundation is needed more, and its members usually have a greater sense of purpose.

Sometimes, the two tracks have to be pursued separately: The local foundation focuses on civil society and I, as the representative of a foreign foundation, deal with the government. Sometimes the second track cannot be pursued at all. Where the local foundation is in charge of both tracks, becoming associated with a particular government can become a problem: The next government may want to undo the work done under the previous one. That is what happened in Hungary and Bulgaria: The foundations got pigeonholed as the ally of a particular party coalition and attracted the hostility of the other one.

Early on, I realized that one of the most important contributions the foundations could make was to improve the capacity of governments at the central and local levels. Civil society is good at criticizing and monitoring, but there has to be something to be monitored and held accountable. We provided training to government employees and offered fellowships to citizens educated abroad to return home and work in the government. We also put foreign experts at the disposal of governments. This strategy filled a gap. The countries we worked in were flooded by foreign experts sent by various foreign countries and international institutions, but they had no suitable counterparts in the government with whom they could interact. We provided governments with foreign experts who would work for them and not for the donors. They could deal with the representatives of international institutions as equals and move matters forward. Countries such as Ukraine benefited greatly from this approach. The only trouble with using foreign experts is that they come and go; to capture their expertise permanently, we set up policy institutes staffed with locals who acted as assistants and, we hoped, retained some of the knowledge when the foreign experts left.

During the chaotic early days we acted on our own, and usually I was personally involved. But that was inappropriate in normal times, so we formed partnerships with, among others, the United Nations Development Programme (UNDP) and institutionalized our assistance. UNDP was also engaged in similar efforts on its own in various countries. Perhaps its most successful initiative was in Nigeria, where President Olusegun Obasanjo wanted to bring back a World Bank official, Ngozi Okonjo-Iweala, to become minister of finance, and, for a transitional period, UNDP paid her World Bank salary (she has children in private schools in America for whose education she has to pay). Vested interests threatened by reforms seized on this issue to criticize the arrangement, but Ngozi was worth her weight in gold.

In cooperation with UNDP, I set up capacity building funds in several countries, including Georgia, after the Revolution of the Roses in 2003, when President Eduard Schevardnadze's regime fell. The fund paid $1,200 a month to government ministers and a subsidy to policemen. This allowed President Mikhail Saakashvili to attract qualified people to the government and to remove the police roadblocks that regularly extorted money from the occupants of passing vehicles. This gave the public a sense that things were going to change for the better. Although the scheme was administered by UNDP, I was subjected to a vicious propaganda campaign orchestrated by Russia. I was accused of having the Georgian government in my pay. Both UNDP and I believe that capacity building funds can be very effective, but they need to be turned into institutions equipped with well-established rules and procedures in order to avoid the criticism to which they have been exposed in the past. Liberia is the first candidate for such a fund.

The Warsaw Declaration of 2000

Private initiatives such as mine are one thing; government intervention in the internal affairs of other countries is quite another. The present world order is built on the twin principles of sovereignty and nonintervention, although these principles are often observed only in the breech. We need to clarify matters. The principle to be established is that it is in the collective interest of all democracies to foster the development of democracy in all other countries. The principle was actually incorporated in the Warsaw Declaration of 2000 and signed by 107 states (a number larger than the number of real democracies in the world), but, like most such declarations, it was an empty gesture.

The principle can be justified on several grounds. First, in our increasingly interdependent world, what goes on inside countries can infringe on the vital interests of other countries. The Taliban and al Qaeda in Afghanistan posed a national security threat to the United States. Second, freedom and democracy are a universal human aspiration. Third, it is also an essential ingredient in economic development, as Amartya Sen has shown in his book *Development as Freedom*.* Fourth, although democracy is an internal affair, it often requires a helping hand from outside. Some governments lack capacity, others are intent on preserving themselves in power. People are often unable to protect themselves against repression; outside intervention may be their only lifeline. What, then, are the rules that ought to govern outside intervention?

The Responsibility to Protect

We must distinguish between constructive and punitive interventions. There is no conflict between constructive intervention, exemplified by my foundations, and the principle of national sovereignty because the countries concerned accept it voluntarily. It is when a government rejects outside support over which it cannot exercise control that the problems begin.

A doctrine has emerged to justify punitive intervention. It is called "the responsibility to protect." It holds that sovereignty belongs to the people; the people entrust it to the government. When the government abuses that trust and violates the human rights of the people, the international

*Amartya Sen, *Development as Freedom* (New York: Alfred A. Knopf, 1999).

community has a responsibility to protect the people. The doctrine has begun to gain some recognition, falling short of full acceptance, in the United Nations, but it raises two problems: First, who constitutes the international community? Second, the doctrine can be applied only to cases of the gravest human rights violations. What can be done in less severe and therefore more hopeful cases?

Since the doctrine has been mooted within the United Nations, the obvious institution to represent the international community is the United Nations. Unfortunately, the United Nations can rarely agree; therefore it is conceivable that a coalition outside the United Nations has to act on behalf of the international community. That was the case in Kosovo, where NATO took the lead. That worked because it had the tacit support of Russia, which would have felt obliged to veto a resolution in the Security Council. Russia played a key role in persuading Slobodan Milosevic to cave in without a fight.

I supported, indeed encouraged, NATO intervention, first in Bosnia and then in Kosovo, but I was passionately opposed to the invasion of Iraq. That is because the United States acted unilaterally and arbitrarily and by doing so undermined the legitimacy of the international community for future interventions. Already Kosovo was a borderline case; Iraq was definitely a violation of international law and discredited the emerging principle of the responsibility to protect.

It is ironic, but the invasion of Iraq has made it more difficult to deal with the likes of Saddam Hussein. Saddam was a heinous tyrant, and most people would agree that it is good to be rid of him. But there are many other tyrants in the world: Kim Jong-il in North Korea, Tan Shwe in Myanmar,

Robert Mugabe in Zimbabwe, Saparmurat Niyazov the Turkmenbashi in Turkmenistan, Islam Karimov in Uzbekistan, and Bashar Assad in Syria, just to mention the worst offenders against human rights. What we should do about the likes of Saddam is one of the great unsolved problems of the prevailing world order, and the invasion of Iraq has taken us further from a solution.

The international community has been in disarray since the invasion of Iraq. Anything proposed by the United States is treated with the utmost suspicion and opposed almost reflexively by other countries; at the same time, the United States is represented in the United Nations by John Bolton, Dick Cheney's protégé, who wants to turn the United Nations into a tool of the United States. As a result, the United Nations has practically ground to a standstill: There has been no progress on the Millennium Development Goals; the proposal to create a Human Rights Council passed only with the greatest difficulty over the almost solitary opposition of the United States; and much needed administrative reforms have been opposed because they were proposed by the United States. America must undergo a fundamental change in behavior before the responsibility to protect can be properly exercised.

Constructive Engagement

Even if the United States managed to reestablish its position as leader of the international community, the second problem would remain. The responsibility to protect applies only in extreme cases; but how can pressure be applied in milder cases? A simple principle suggests itself: We ought to do much more on the constructive side. Constructive engagement does not violate the principle of sovereignty and, most important, the withdrawal of assistance does not violate it, either. The more we do on the constructive side, the more options we have in imposing penalties. Moreover, democratic development badly needs outside assistance. I have been arguing the case ever since I became involved in fostering open societies, but to no avail. I set up my foundations in countries such as Ukraine in the hope that others would follow, but when I looked back, no one was behind me. On the contrary, the prevailing world order is biased in the opposite direction. I attribute it to the prevalence of market fundamentalism. Providing assistance goes against the grain, but imposing market discipline is right in line.

A change of heart by the United States will involve more than accepting the unique responsibility of world leadership; it will require a rethinking of the role of markets and the role of government at home as well. The United States cannot lead constructive engagement abroad without engaging in it at home.

A Fundamentalist Fallacy

This raises a question: What role should governments play in the economy? Market fundamentalists want to remove government from the economy altogether, and they hate international institutions even more than domestic ones. The trouble is that market fundamentalists are right when they assert that governments are ill-suited to run the economy and that is even more true in the international arena than in the domestic one. Foreign aid has been notoriously ineffective. More generally, it is the shortcomings of governments as economic actors that has led to the rise of market fundamentalism. Am I now advocating a return to government intervention in the economy on an international scale?

I believe it is a mistake to pose this as an either/or question. There is a need for some government intervention both internally and internationally, even if governments are ill-suited to run the economy. The distortions and inefficiencies introduced by government regulations can be kept to a minimum by using incentives and penalties that work through the market mechanism. Let the markets do what they do best, namely, allocate resources; but make sure that the collective needs that would normally be ignored by markets as externalities get proper recognition in the allocation process.

Government regulations and markets both have their strengths and weaknesses. The fact that one is imperfect does not render the other perfect. That is the fallacy in all fundamentalism: fundamentalists crave certainty and perfect solutions. When an arrangement fails, they expect its opposite to be perfect. I am equally opposed to market fundamentalism and government ownership or control over productive resources. I do believe, however, that the pendulum has swung too far towards market fundamentalism. As I mentioned before, globalization has been a market fundamentalist project. Communism and even milder forms of government control have been discredited; that is why I pay less attention to their deficiencies.

Shortcomings of Foreign Aid

The shortcomings of constructive engagement by governments can be best appreciated by comparing them with my foundations. Two features stand out. Governments tend to give preference to their national interests, or the interests of their nationals, over the interests of the people whom they are supposed to assist. This can be seen in the way foreign aid is administered: The interests of the donors take precedence over the interests of the recipients. Governments are also more attuned to dealing with other governments than with nongovernmental organizations. The World Bank and the International Monetary Fund are required by their constitutions to obtain government guarantees. As a result, the assistance tends to bolster the role of governments in the economy, and the aid may never reach the people, particularly under repressive, corrupt, or inept regimes.

That is not to say that my foundations are perfect. They proceed by way of trial and error, and errors abound. I am ready to accept errors and to abandon projects when they fail. This gives us a comparative advantage. Bureaucracies find it difficult to admit failure; this makes them risk-averse. We can tolerate risks; therefore we can reap greater rewards. Another major factor working in our favor is that the people engaged in the foundations are genuinely concerned about the welfare of the recipients. This feature could be replicated in official organizations. If an organization is dedicated to a specific mission, the people employed by it are generally guided by that mission. That is true of the International Monetary Fund as well as the Global Fund to Fight AIDS, Tuberculosis and Malaria. The key is to define the mission well and to give the institution the independence and the resources it needs.

I am particularly keen on the Global Fund to Fight AIDS, Tuberculosis and Malaria. It has a well-defined and worthy mission and it uses many of the same methods as my foundations. It has a small staff, it invites proposals from nongovernmental as well as governmental sources, and it makes awards based on merit, not on quotas. It has the courage to suspend projects when conditions are violated, and it is ready to reexamine and improve its own operations. Unfortunately, it is not getting adequate funding. In the beginning, the Bush administration overcame its aversion to international organizations and supported the Global Fund. That was due to the remarkable success of Bono, the rock-singer, who mobilized religious communities in favor of fighting AIDS. But the administration set up its own program, PEPFAR (President's Emergency Plan for HIV/AIDS Relief). The total amount devoted to fighting AIDS has increased, but the Bush administration no longer contributes its fair share to the Global Fund.

How to make constructive interventions more effective is a complicated subject. I do not want to get bogged down in details, especially as I dealt with the subject elsewhere.* The point I want to make here is that we need more and earlier constructive interventions. The present world order is slanted in favor of nonintervention and punitive action.

The Case for Promoting Open Societies

By the time punitive intervention is contemplated, it is usually too late. When a regime goes too far in a repressive

*George Soros, *The Bubble of American Supremacy* (New York: PublicAffairs, 2003).

direction, the international community has very little leverage left. Take the case of Mugabe in Zimbabwe or Karimov in Uzbekistan: They continue to commit atrocities and the international community is powerless to stop them. Less-repressive regimes can be overturned by revolution. That is the lesson of the so-called color revolutions in Georgia, Ukraine, and Kyrgyzstan: If you want to run a repressive regime, you had better be ruthless. To prevent this lesson from spreading in the world, constructive intervention ought to start sooner and make its effect felt on a much larger scale. Constructive intervention cannot start early enough. Since in the early stages it is impossible to predict which situation will culminate in a regime that is beyond redemption, the best recipe is to foster democratic development wherever possible.

The Bush administration's policies are full of contradictions. President Bush argued against "nation building" in the television debate of the 2000 elections, and nation building was furthest from his mind when he ordered the invasion of Afghanistan. We had a chance to make a successful demonstration of democratic development in Afghanistan, but we failed to rise to the occasion. Yet we advocate democratization in other countries.

In an article published in the *Washington Post*, I tried to explain how to do it in Afghanistan.* We should have distributed aid directly to the communities, paying the salaries of teachers, judges, and other officials on behalf of the central government. The United Nations was well-represented on the ground in Afghanistan with several hundred employees

*George Soros, "Assembling Afghanistan," *Washington Post*, December 3, 2001.

who knew their way around. If we had sent troops under the aegis of the United Nations to guard the money that was being distributed, they would have been welcome and the authority of the central government would have been firmly established. But that was alien to the Bush administration's thinking. As it is, we formed alliances with warlords, and it is their authority that we helped to establish; in this way, we consolidated an economic and political system based on the illegal cultivation of narcotics.*

There is a confusion in President Bush's mind about what democracy means. When he says that democracy will prevail, he really means that America will prevail. But a democratic government needs to gain the backing of the electorate and that is not necessarily the same as the backing of the United States. The contradiction became evident in the recent elections in Egypt, and even more in Palestine. After the victory of Hamas, the Bush administration is likely to revise and quietly abandon its program of democratization in the Greater Middle East. That would be a pity, though, because several countries are caught in quandaries from which they cannot extricate themselves without democratic development.

The victory of Hamas is considered a defeat for the policy of

*I took practical measures to back up my opinions. My foundation provided seed money to a working group led by Ashraf Ghani, an Afghan World Bank official, and Barnett R. Rubin, an American expert on Afghanistan, to make plans for a political transition. They played an important role in preparing the Bonn conference and the Loya Jirga, which laid the legal foundations for a democratic state. Ashraf Ghani then became finance minister and we set up a capacity-building fund under his supervision to attract other expatriates to return to Afghanistan and work in the government. Ashraf Ghani lost his job after the elections and eventually the fund ran its course and was not refinanced. We continue to support civil society through groups such as the Foundation for Culture and Civil Society. Of course, these meager efforts were not able to make much difference to the way events unfolded. Ghani is now director of the University of Kabul.

promoting democracy. I take a different view. Free elections help to clarify matters even if they bring the wrong people to power.

I have not been closely involved in Israeli affairs, but once I visited Israel at the invitation of Prime Minister Yitzhak Rabin just as the peace talks were at their zenith. Rabin was talking with Yasser Arafat on the cell phone during dinner and the mood was euphoric. I asked Rabin whether there was any chance of including Hamas in the agreement. I told him of my experience in Poland, where I had a private dinner with Wojciech Jaruzelski on the occasion of setting up a foundation there *before* the settlement with Solidarity. Jaruzelski told me that he was willing to talk with anyone except Solidarity because the leaders of Solidarity were traitors who had called for trade sanctions that left children starving. I said he was mistaken: The leaders of Solidarity were patriots who were willing to sacrifice their own constituency, heavy industry, for the sake of Poland (heavy industry would suffer the most in a market economy). There can be no settlement except with the organization that represents the people. I could see that my argument made an impression on him. With this experience as background, I cannot help believing that an agreement reached with Hamas would be more enduring than one concluded with a Palestinian authority that does not enjoy the trust of the people. The agreement reached with Arafat did not last.

I realize that the point stretches the imagination. The chances of reaching an agreement with Hamas are practically nil. Hamas is not Solidarity: It is a militant Islamist organization and Israel is not in a mood to take chances. Yet I cannot help thinking that with skillful diplomacy there could be an opening to drive a wedge between the homegrown leaders of Hamas who won the election and have an obligation to the people of Palestine to improve their living conditions and the expatriate leadership based in Syria and beholden to Iran.

Or consider another intractable case, Pakistan. President Pervez Musharraf is a very uncertain and unreliable ally: The top leadership of al Qaeda is hiding in Pakistan, and the resurgence of the Taliban is supported by elements within Pakistan. President Musharraf tells us that the choice is between him and the Islamic fundamentalists; with Pakistan in possession of nuclear weapons, that makes the choice obvious. But Musharraf is in alliance with the religious parties; that makes it difficult for him to exert pressure on them. Little effort has been made to reform the madrassahs, and the state spends less than two percent of its budget on education. Even so, the religious parties would probably get only a minority of the votes in free elections. The two moderate parties that alternated in power when the military allowed elections have deep roots in society in spite of all the efforts of the military dictatorship to destroy them. Musharraf dismisses them as corrupt; but the military are no better. Musharraf himself is not as popular as his supporters have us believe; that is why he refuses to carry out his promise to stand for elections; that is why he has to rely on the religious parties. This is a case where free elections could resolve what is presented as an intractable problem. The real problem is how to persuade the military to hold free elections.

Egypt has some similarities with Pakistan, the major difference being that in free elections the Moslem Brotherhood would gain a majority. Then there is the enigma of Saudi Arabia: If that country were opened up, who knows what would be found inside. The fact is, the Middle East has been profoundly messed up by a long history of Western intervention aimed at controlling natural resources, particularly oil, not at building democracies. That is one reason why so few democracies are to be found there.

The situation cannot be changed from one day to the next. Building open societies is a long and arduous process, and it does not necessarily start with free elections. When the population is uneducated and valuable resources are at stake, free elections may be a recipe for instability. Resource rich countries with free elections but without the rule of law have lower rates of growth than autocratic countries.* The Bush administration has chosen the wrong solution for the wrong reason. As the adverse consequences become apparent, the policy is liable to be quietly abandoned. That would be regrettable: Building open societies remains the only promising way forward.

Even if the goal of fostering open societies should survive the Bush administration, the administration's policies will have done lasting damage. The war on terror and the invasion of Iraq have lost America the moral high ground. In addition, they revealed some glaring deficiencies in America as a role model. The rest of the world sees the Bush administration's advocacy of democracy and human rights as a thin cover for American imperialism and speaks of dual standards. This will make it much harder for America to preach freedom and democracy in the future. The aspiration for freedom and democracy will live on, but people will have to carry on the struggle for freedom in spite of President Bush's rhetoric.

*Paul Collier and Anke Hoeffler, "Oil Democracies" (University of Oxford, Department of Economics, June 14, 2005, p. 2)

NUCLEAR PROLIFERATION

I want to mention two other unsolved problems of the current world order: nuclear proliferation and global warming. In the Cold War the best minds on both sides were engaged in figuring out how to ensure that nuclear weapons would not be used. Strategists eventually realized that the existence of large stockpiles of nuclear weapons made nuclear war unthinkable because it would result in Mutually Assured Destruction. The international agreements that followed limited nuclear testing and attempted to implement a worldwide nuclear non-proliferation regime. Even so, we had some close brushes.

The problem that has arisen since the end of the Cold War is much more complicated and there is no solution in sight. Although there are treaties and other arrangements to prevent the proliferation of states with nuclear arms, there are also strong incentives that lead countries to decide to acquire nuclear weapons. A class system has emerged dividing the world into nuclear haves and have nots. The non-proliferation treaty permits only the five states that tested a nuclear device prior to January 1, 1967 to be treated as nuclear powers. All other states are prohibited from developing nuclear weapons, but are guaranteed an "inalienable right" to peaceful nuclear technology. In practice, the three states (India, Pakistan, and Israel) which did not sign the NPT have come to have their nuclear status accepted. India and Pakistan were ostracized for a while, but the world eventually accepted the fait accompli. The same process may now be at work for states which withdraw from the NPT as North Korea has done and Iran might be tempted to do.

The Bush doctrine, asserting America's right to preemptive military action, has reinforced the benefits of becoming a nuclear power: by invading the only member of the "axis of evil" that did not have a nuclear program, Bush has shown that having nuclear weapons exempts you from the Bush doctrine. Although there is an efficient and sophisticated international detection agency, its task has been rendered more difficult by the spread of nuclear know-how. Easier access to nuclear technology—spread by the likes of A.Q. Khan's nuclear network—makes it easier for nations to circumvent international safeguards. The lack of international resolve to move quickly to stop proliferation activities, such as those of A.Q. Khan, also cripples the international non-proliferation regime. In these circumstances, the incentives tend to outweigh the constraints. The more countries acquire nuclear weapons, the greater the pressure on others to do likewise. Regional tensions and nuclear armament in South and East Asia make nuclear weapons appealing for neighbors. Nuclear modernization efforts by the world's two largest nuclear powers heighten the perceived importance of nuclear weapons for national security. The inducements may not be strong enough to push countries to actually violate the non-proliferation treaty, but they have every reason to line up at the starting line. That is where a number of countries are heading. In addition to North Korea and Iran, countries such as Argentina, Brazil, and Japan are believed to have the capacity to use their peaceful nuclear technology to produce weapons-grade material if they chose to do so. Estimates are that, outside the nine countries that have produced nuclear weapons, up to 40 countries could produce nuclear weapons if they were willing to devote the necessary resources. Only the ever-thinning taboo against nuclear weapons possession remains between these nuclear-capable states and nuclear weapons.

Although the spread of nuclear weapons constitutes a threat to humanity, the arguments for non-proliferation are undermined by the fact that the nuclear weapon states have not fulfilled their obligations under the non-proliferation pact: they have made only very limited moves toward complete disarmament, as required by Article VI of the NPT. Moreover, the United States maintains the option to develop new nuclear weapons and is mixing nuclear and conventional weapons in national defense policy, the Bush administration's new concept of integrated defense, the New Triad, severely lowering the bar for deciding to use nuclear weapons. The United States is also continuing to assert the right to use nuclear weapons whenever it chooses.

The situation is much more dangerous than at any time in the Cold War, yet much less thought is given to the subject than during the Cold War. The best brains are not engaged. Insofar as there is public discussion, it is focused on weapons of mass destruction falling into the hands of terrorists. This is an obfuscation. The very term "Weapons of Mass Destruction" is misleading, because it lumps together weapons with very different characteristics. The most potent threat, in my opinion, is the proliferation of nuclear weapons in the hands of states. That threat is not receiving the attention it deserves.

There is little hope for a solution while the United States is modernizing its strategic arsenal and continuing to have plans to use nuclear weapons. A solution could only exist if a new non-proliferation agreement were negotiated—a new non-proliferation treaty that would put *all* nuclear programs under international supervision. It would not deprive the United States and other states of their weapons, but it would place them under international monitoring to ensure immediate detection if a country decided to initiate the use of nuclear weapons. But since there are plentiful amounts of highly enriched uranium already in existence, it is possible for nations to acquire fissile materials without producing their own. The other necessary treaty component must therefore implement international control of the production and disposal of the fissile materials necessary to build nuclear weapons. Such an arrangement would run counter to the prevailing view that American sovereignty is sacrosanct but it could make the world, us included, a safer place.

The United States believes that Iran is hell-bent on acquiring nuclear weapons and Iran has done nothing to discredit this notion. The world is heading toward a confrontation. Only the timing is uncertain. As I mentioned in the previous chapter, I believe it may be possible to reach an accommodation with Iran but it ought not to permit Iran to become a nuclear power. Iran has been the main beneficiary of the invasion of Iraq but if it overplays its hand it may lose all the benefits. If Iraq deteriorates into a regional Shia-Sunni confrontation, Iran is liable to be drawn into it. A commitment by the United States to withdraw its troops could serve both as a threat (because it would leave the United States free to bomb Iran's nuclear installations) and as an inducement to cooperate in a political settlement (because it would consolidate the gains Iran has already made without risking them in a war.) Iran has suffered greatly during eight years of fighting with Saddam Hussein and another war may not appeal to at least some segments of the power structure. Giving up the nuclear program may not be much of a sacrifice especially if the international community were willing to enter into a new nonproliferation agreement that would put all existing nuclear weapons under an international regime and impose a freeze on all further development of nuclear capabilities. If most of the world were lined up behind such a treaty, Iran would find it difficult to resist, and if it did, preemptive action by the United States would encounter fewer adverse consequences than at present.

GLOBAL WARMING

Another problem whose solution requires international cooperation is global warming. I am a relatively recent convert to the cause. I used to think that I had too much on my plate already so I had better leave environmental issues to others. But global warming has begun to loom so large that I can no longer ignore it. I was moved by former Vice President Al Gore's persuasive presentation. I checked it out with scientists, and they confirmed that scientific opinion is unanimous about the dangers; they only differ on the speed of the process. There are many delayed effects; indeed, even if all new carbon emissions stopped today, the warming of the oceans would continue for some time. Average temperatures are already higher than at any time in human history, so further warming poses a real threat to the survival of human civilization. The situation is not hopeless because we are likely to be more adaptable than we think, but the danger is real and there is no time to waste.

Unfortunately, the Bush administration is in denial. Public opinion is well ahead of the administration on global warming, but there is a lot of confusion and obfuscation by special interests. Exxon-Mobil has been the main sponsor of advocacy groups whose goal is to confuse the public. Peer-reviewed scientific publications are unanimous on the existence of a serious manmade problem; reports in public media, however, are evenly divided. That is the achievement of these advocacy groups. Nevertheless, cities and states are taking action on their own; only federal action is missing.

The international community agreed on the Kyoto Protocol in 1997, and President Clinton signed on in the final days of his presidency. President Bush renounced the Protocol soon after he was elected, and he never proposed any real alternative in its place. He promised to develop hydrogen as an alternative clean fuel, but there is no proven technology, and even if there were, it would take too long to develop; so that was only an excuse for inaction. There is general agreement that the Kyoto Protocol is inadequate, but it is a useful starting point. The Protocol does not apply to developing countries, but China and India are developing so fast that they will have to be included in the next round. Moreover, the targets have been set too low because the trading in pollution rights that the Protocol has spawned has a built-in bias that rewards those who reduce emissions without penalizing those who increase it. For instance, you can earn brownie points for producing ethanol, but the burning or clearing of tropical forests is not counted against you. Thus the Kyoto Protocol targets could be met without significantly slowing global warming.

Although the Kyoto Protocol came into force without U.S. participation, future progress hinges on a change of attitude by the United States. Plans are afoot to mobilize U.S. public opinion, and I hope that will make a difference.

Economic Prospects

The global economy is on an even keel at the time of this writing. There are some fundamental imbalances, of which the United States trade deficit and the Asian trade surpluses are the most glaring, but these may continue indefinitely because a willing borrower is matched by willing lenders. There are no signs of a financial crisis, and global markets have been remarkably resilient in absorbing shocks such as the rise in the price of oil. The financial authorities are reinforced in their belief that with proper supervision financial markets can take care of themselves. Perhaps the only cloud on the horizon is that some developing countries, such as Indonesia, South Africa, and various Latin American countries, are not developing fast enough to satisfy the aspirations of the people; thus the stage is set for political discontent, but the international financial authorities do not feel qualified to address the problem.

I do not think the current calm is going to last. As I mentioned earlier, I believe the global economy has been sustained by a housing boom that took on the characteristics of a bubble. In some countries, notably the United Kingdom and Australia, the bubble has subsided, but no serious dislocations have resulted. Consumer spending fell, but even a modest decline in interest rates was sufficient to stabilize house prices and consumer spending. This is called a soft landing and it has encouraged the authorities to think that the same will happen in the United States. I take a different view. There are reasons to believe that the slowdown in housing prices in the United States will see repercussions more severe than in other countries. One reason is the sheer size of the United States economy. A slowdown in the United States will reverberate in the global economy, but Australia and the United Kingdom are too small for a slowdown to have much effect. Another factor is that in the United States the rise in prices was accompanied by a rise in the volume of new construction, whereas in the United Kingdom new construction remained stable. This has created an overhang of excess supply in the United States that will take time to work off. Finally, lending standards in the United States have been relaxed more than elsewhere, and they are in the process of being tightened. All these factors combined are likely to ensure that housing prices, once they subside, will not rise again soon. As I have discussed earlier, I expect an initial soft landing to turn into a hard one when the slowdown does not end. A slowdown in the United States will be transmitted to the rest of the world via a weaker dollar. That is why I expect a worldwide slowdown starting in 2007.

I may be wrong, of course. I have been wrong before. It may be unwise to go on record with this particular thesis because once it is in print, it is difficult to retract or modify. I am putting it forward as an illustration of the kind of dislocation that is bound to occur sooner or later. The point I am trying to make is that the global economy is prone to periodic dislocations and it will require international cooperation to keep them within bounds.

Even in the absence of a crisis there is something perverse in the current constellation: The savings of the world are sucked up to the center to finance overconsumption by the richest and largest country, the United States. This cannot continue indefinitely, and when it stops the global economy will suffer from a deficiency of demand. The Asian countries that are financing U.S. overconsumption would be well-advised to stimulate domestic consumption, but even if they succeeded there may be a temporary shortfall. It would behoove the international financial authorities to engage in contingency planning, but I see no sign of it.* In the past, I have proposed that the International Monetary Fund could issue Special Drawing Rights (SDRs), the rich countries assigning their allocations for international assistance. There are technical difficulties—assigning SDRs would require budget allocations—but if my expectation of a global slowdown in 2007 turns out to be correct, it is a scheme whose time may have come.

Conclusion

Enough has been said to show that the prevailing world order is confronted by unsolved problems. Some of them, such as nuclear proliferation and global warming, could endanger our civilization; others are less cataclysmic. Our civilization has seen many tyrants and many financial crises and it has survived them all. Nevertheless, the world would be a better place if some progress could be made on these issues. That would require a greater degree of international cooperation than is possible at present. The responsibility lies with

*This statement is no longer valid, due to the G7 communiqué on April 22, 2006.

the United States. The United States needs to regain its position as the legitimate leader of the free world not only for its own sake but also for the sake of the world. A world order based on the sovereignty of states requires the leadership of a sovereign state that is powerful enough to occupy that position and farsighted enough to pay attention to the common interests of an interdependent world. American leadership has not always been enlightened, but the United States is at present the only country that could qualify for the position.

To become the legitimate leader of the free world, the United States will have to do more than just revert to the policies it followed before 9/11. It would have to pursue a truly humble foreign policy, respecting the opinion of others and paying attention to their interests. It cannot be done by a feel-good society. I am afraid that America is not ready to resist the manipulation of truth that characterizes the political process, nor is it prepared to subordinate its narrowly perceived self-interests to a greater common interest. As a result, the United States is unlikely to regain its leadership position. Already during the past five years America has lost more ground than seemed conceivable at the time the Bush doctrine was promulgated. This raises the question of how the stability of the world order can be preserved when American dominance fades. It leads me to consider the role of Europe, the community of democracies and international civil society.

CHAPTER 6

Exploring the Alternatives

Under the Bush administration, the United States has failed to exercise the leadership role it has occupied, with more or less success, since World War Two. Where could the leadership that the world needs come from? The only sovereign entity that can come into consideration is the European Union, but it is undergoing its own crisis of identity. China is coming up fast, but if it tried to lead the world, it would run into implacable opposition, especially from the United States. Without some common ground, a world order based on the sovereignty of states is bound to deteriorate into disorder; indeed, it is happening now because the most powerful nation on earth, the United States, has aroused the hostility of the world. This hostility paralyzes the international institutions we have—and the institutions we have are not strong enough to start with.

No sovereign entity can replace the United States in the foreseeable future, but the United States will have been severely weakened by the eight years of George W. Bush's presidency. Unfortunately, the next administration, even if it seeks to recapture the position the United States held previously, will find it difficult to do so. It will have to rely on international cooperation to a greater extent than previously. Its preferred partners ought to be the European Union, the broader community of democracies and international civil society. I shall consider each of them in turn.

THE EUROPEAN UNION

I have always considered the European Union the embodiment of the open society idea. It has been brought into existence by piecemeal social engineering—Popper's favored method for improving the world—based on the recognition that perfection is unattainable. Each step was designed to achieve a limited goal within a limited timeframe, fully understanding that the new arrangement will prove inadequate and necessitate a further step forward. That is how the European Union was constructed, one step at a time.

The result is an association of states that have agreed to a limited delegation of sovereignty. The degree of delegation takes a variety of forms, and memberships of various institutions like the European Central Bank and the Schengen Zone overlap. There is no grand design. The European Union is a collection of nationalities in which no nationality has a majority. These are the features that make the European Union the prototype of an open society. But it is still a work in progress, and in its unfinished state the European Union suffers from several deficiencies: It is too unwieldy for the size of its membership, it is opaque and bureaucratic, and the democratic influence is too indirect, so that people feel alienated. The dissatisfaction found expression in the recent rejection of the European Constitution by French and Dutch voters.

The construction of the European Union has now missed a step. The political will moving the process forward has run out of steam. Admittedly, conditions have changed since the Cold War. The Communist threat has dissipated, and globalization has become the dominant influence in the world. Globalization has rendered the welfare state, established in the aftermath of the Second World War, unsustainable in its original form. European attitudes towards globalization are sharply divided. Some want to use the European Union to preserve the achievements of the welfare state by creating a fortress Europe; others want to use it to force European economies to become more competitive. Yet others see the European Union as globalization writ small and therefore a threat to the welfare state they want to protect.

It is not only the movement of capital that has created problems but also the movement of people. The proverbial Polish plumber taking your job, the prospect of Turkish membership, and the growth of Muslim, African, and Asian immigrant communities all contributed to the resentment that led to the rejection of the Constitution. But the current crisis also raises questions about the viability of the open society concept. The European Union is proving less alluring as a fact than it was as an aspiration. That is a characteristic of open societies in general.

The crisis is not terminal. The European Union will be sustained by what has been considered one of its deficiencies: bureaucratic inertia. Decisions require consensus; in the absence of consensus, past decisions remain in force. That will keep the European Union going for a while. Instead of crisis, it may be more appropriate to speak of stasis. But in a fast-changing world, organizations that cannot make decisions cannot survive indefinitely. Therefore, the European Union must be revived if it is to survive.

One thing is certain: The process that has carried the European Union forward so far cannot be revived in the same form as before. It was driven by an elite, and the population at large has felt left out. This cannot continue, if for no other reason than on account of the referenda that are used with increasing frequency. Referenda express the people's will in a raw, capricious form without the intermediation of an elite. Therefore, if the European Union is to revive, it has to be by popular demand. That demand is missing, and an abstract idea such as the open society cannot generate it. Open society can serve as a political goal in a repressive society, but not in an open one. The abstract idea has to be filled with concrete content, and when it comes to content, the people of Europe are sharply divided. They have not even decided whether or not the European Union should be a military power. And they are at loggerheads in their attitudes towards globalization.

The absence of the European Union as a military power compounds the disarray in the prevailing world order. That already nebulous entity, the West, has become even more nebulous. In the absence of a cohesive international community, there is no legitimate authority to exercise the responsibility to protect. As a result, tyrants reign with impunity in other parts of the world and the victims of repressive regimes and failed states remain unprotected.

Herein lies an idea that might propel the European Union forward: the idea of a global open society that needs the European Union as its prototype. The European Union has a mission: the spread of peace, freedom, and democracy. Not unlike the Bush agenda but hopefully better founded, the European Union has been more successful in carrying out that mission than most people realize. The prospect of membership has been the most powerful tool in turning candidate countries into open societies. Therefore, the European Union must, in principle, remain open to new members if it is to fulfill its mission.

Is this idea strong enough to serve as a unifying force driving the European Union forward? It is certainly strong enough for me. Although I am not a European citizen, I consider myself a European patriot, and I have a network of foundations, inside and outside the European Union, that regard membership in the European Union as their main objective. Could this be the basis of a popular movement?

The answer has to be no. As I have already mentioned, open society is too abstract an idea to generate popular support. The masses are concerned with prosperity and security, not with foreign policy. But Europe as the prototype of a global open society could fire the imagination of a minority whose engagement might counteract the influence of those motivated by nationalist and racist sentiments. The advantage of activating a pro-open-society minority is that they would not have to agree on other issues currently dividing Europe. Social democrats, Christian democrats, and liberal democrats could all unite behind the foreign policy mission of the European Union.

The European Union is facing a test, namely, the membership negotiations with Turkey. Is the abstract idea of an open society stronger than the prejudices against a Muslim country that once threatened to conquer Christian Europe?

The current outlook is not encouraging: Extremists on both sides are aggravating prejudices. When the famous Turkish novelist Orhan Pamuk was put on trial in Turkey, it was not the government that was responsible but rather recalcitrant elements within the Turkish state structures who wanted to embarrass the government. When a Danish newspaper recently published caricatures of the Prophet it may have been an innocent prank, but the domestic Moslem minority took it as a provocation. The Danish prime minister, Anders Fogh Rasmussen, catering to his own constituency, refused to meet the ambassadors of Arab countries who sought to warn him of impending trouble. Syria and Iran had their own reasons for promoting angry reactions. Subsequently, riots spread through most of the Moslem world. Unfortunately, when extremists play off each other, the general public becomes polarized. I saw it happen in the Balkans and later in the war on terror. Now it is happening in Europe with the clash of Moslem and anti-Moslem sensibilities.

In theory, it should not be too difficult to keep the negotiations with Turkey alive. Turkey is not meant to become a member of the European Union right away; the process will probably take at least ten years. But strong political forces are seeking to terminate the process by making the position of the Turkish government untenable. Cyprus is the weapon. The island has been divided for decades, and the Greek side recently became a member of the European Union. It is now using its membership to obstruct the reunification plan that has been devised by the United Nations and agreed to by the Turkish side. Cyprus is aided and abetted by European politicians such as Nicholas Sarkozy in France and the foreign minister of Austria, Ursula Plassnik, who would like the negotiations to break down. The European Union is now demanding one-sided concessions from a Turkish government that is under countervailing pressure from domestic forces opposed to European membership. The European Union wants Turkey to admit ships from Cyprus; Turkey wants the European Union to open trade with Turkish Northern Cyprus which Cyprus, as a member of the European Union is able to block. Unless the other members put sufficient pressure on Cyprus, the accession process is liable to break down. The consequences could be far-reaching. If the prospect of membership is removed, the incipient civil war in Iraq could also destabilize Turkey. Already a splinter group of Kurdish nationalists is fomenting trouble in Eastern Turkey.

If negotiations with Turkey are suspended, the future of Europe may be decided sooner than we think and it may be decided without the general public realizing what the stakes are. What is worse, even if the public were aware of the issues, they may not line up behind the idea of Europe as an open society. The idea has not been given sufficient content to excite people's enthusiasm. Instead of looking forward towards an uncertain, confusing and threatening future, people are looking backwards and seeking solace in their national or local identities. But the past history of Europe is full of wars and the wars have a tendency to become ever more devastating. That is not an alluring prospect. It is better to face forward even if the future is full of uncertainties. The task is to clarify the confusion. Recognizing our fallibility is not enough; we must also find a way to assure the survival of our civilization. Speaking in very general terms, it is clear that the world needs a greater degree of cooperation than the United States is currently willing to foster. That is the mission for a stronger and more cohesive European Union.

European countries have a different attitude towards co-operation than the United States. Robert Kagan wrote in his book *Of Paradise and Power* that Europeans are from Venus, Americans from Mars.* His argument was neo-Marxist in the sense that he derived the ideological superstructure from the different material conditions that prevail in the United States and Europe. The United States is the sole remaining superpower, but Europe has not even decided whether to become a military power. Europeans dislike the use of military force, while the United States under the Bush administration revels in it. Europeans are aware of the common needs of humanity, and they are willing to make some sacrifices for it. They devote a much larger portion of their national income to foreign aid than the United States, and they have subscribed to the Kyoto Protocol against global warming.[†]

The attitude of the Bush administration has had disastrous consequences; the world needs an alternative and the European Union can provide it. To capture people's imagination, the mission must be spelled out in greater detail. Some of the major controversies that currently divide opinion need to be resolved. Should the European Union be a power or an association of powers? How does the European Union relate to globalization? Should the European Union be open to additional membership? Should it be open to immigration?

---

*Robert Kagan, *Of Paradise and Power: America and Europe in the New World Order* (New York: Alfred A. Knopf, 2003).

[†]But private foundations in the U.S., benefiting from favorable tax rules, contribute a lot more than European foundations.

It is not for me as an outsider to resolve these questions. But as a believer in the open society, I see the direction that Europe ought to take quite clearly: It ought to become the prototype of a global open society. That means recognizing that we belong to a global society and that our common interests ought to hold us together. It also means recognizing that globalization as it is practiced now is a lopsided, distorted version of a global open society. We need global institutions to match global markets. We need to resist the penetration of market values into areas of activity where they do not belong. At the same time, we must exclude governments from a direct role in managing the economy. The role of governments and international institutions is to set the rules, and it is the role of economic agents to compete within those rules. The rules ought to serve the common interest; competitors ought to pursue their own interests; but the competitors ought not to be allowed to bend the rules to suit their own interests. This is, of course, an impossible goal, similar to the Marxist ideal of everybody contributing according to his ability and receiving according to his needs. How close we can come to the ideal depends on our values and attitudes.

America has cultivated competition and carried it to unsustainable extremes. Europe comes from a tradition of cooperation. The influence of the community was at times so overwhelming that individuals sought to escape from it; that is one reason so many emigrated to America. Nevertheless, Europe has a tradition worth cultivating. People still believe in social justice on the Continent and in fair play in England. That is a good base to build on.

How do these noble sentiments translate into practical

policies? The European Union needs to be competitive, but it can try to make the rules more equitable. To this end, it must be a power in a world of sovereign states, not just an association of powers. With an aging population, immigration is an economic necessity. As the prototype of a global open society, Europe needs to be open to immigration and to membership, but not without constraints. Sequencing is important. The issues of governance need to be settled before further enlargement, but for the sake of maintaining peace in the neighborhood, the principle of enlargement cannot be abandoned. That applies to Turkey in particular. Negotiations must continue, but, as I mentioned earlier, they will last a long time. That leaves time to settle the issues of governance. That is about as far as the general principles of open society can carry me. The rest is up to the Europeans. Let the debate begin! As I shall explain in greater detail in the next chapter, Europe's dependence on Russian gas might be a good opening topic. The countries of Europe need to cooperate to ensure their energy security.

The European Union that will emerge from the discussions is liable to be somewhat antagonistic towards the United States, at least under its current leadership; but if it is successful, it is likely to influence the direction that the United States and other democracies take. That would help reconstitute the international community that the world so badly needs.

Can the people of Europe be inspired by this mission? The auguries are ambiguous. European countries have become feel-good societies, and in this respect they are just like the United States. There is not that much difference between them as far as consumerism and a lack of intrinsic values is concerned. On the other hand, creating a prototype for a global open society could make you feel really good. It is worth trying.

THE COMMUNITY OF DEMOCRACIES

A community of democracies that would exercise the responsibility to protect is an attractive idea in theory, but it has been disappointing in practice. The idea was launched in the waning days of the Clinton administration, in the summer of 2000, at a conference held in Warsaw. From the outset, the initiative suffered because it was a product of the foreign ministries and lacked support from the ministries of finance. As a result, the Warsaw Declaration has remained an empty gesture; it would not even have made it into the newspapers if France had not refused to sign it because it had been sponsored by the United States.

The Warsaw Declaration calls for biannual conferences to review progress. I have attended two of them so far, but I found them frustrating. In theory, the format is very attractive because it brings the governmental and nongovernmental sides together. In practice, nothing happens. The discussion revolves around a new declaration that is equally inconsequential but whose text is fought over by diplomats as if it mattered. The last meeting, in Chile in April 2005, was especially frustrating because the community of democracies could not agree about endorsing the proposed Human Rights Council. Many developing democracies were suspicious that the United States would use the Human Rights Council to further its imperial goals. This confirmed my contention that the United States has lost its ability to lead the world. Subsequently, the General Assembly of the United Nations approved the Human Rights Council against the almost solitary opposition of the United States. This event offers an opportunity for the community of democracies to take on real significance by ensuring that only democracies are elected to the Council. That is easier said than done because UN elections are the outcome of intricate bargaining, and individual countries have many interests other than their membership in the Community of Democracies. For instance, it would be next to impossible to keep Cuba off the Council. Nevertheless, the Community of Democracies could exert real influence not only on which countries are elected but also on how the Council functions. The foundation's support of the Community of Democracies could finally begin to pay off.

If the United States changed its attitude, the Community of Democracies could become an influential factor both within the United Nations and beyond. At present, sponsorship by the United States would practically assure resistance by other democracies, particularly among the developing countries. Another administration could take on the leadership position but it would have to recognize that there are just too many divergent interests between the developing and developed democracies for them to be united into a single organization. It would be better if each had its own association, the two cooperating when their interests coincided. This is partly reflected in the current global architecture with a Group of Seven (G–7) and a Group of Twenty (G–20). The developing democracies already started forming their own association when the representatives of twenty-one developing countries met in Cancun in September 2003 to protect their interests in connection with the World Trade Organization negotiations.

The clash between the developed and developing worlds has derailed the Doha Round of trade talks. The United States, under a different president, could demonstrate its change of heart by encouraging the formation of a community of developing democracies, to which the United States and the members of the European Union would *not* belong. This could replace the Group of 77 (G–77) nonaligned nations that currently operate as a faction within the United Nations. Nonaligned with whom? The G–77 has outlived its usefulness. A community of developing democracies in alliance with the United States and Europe would then constitute a governing majority within the United Nations, but they would not necessarily agree on all issues.

At present, the developed countries condescend to the developing ones. For instance, the Group of 8 (G–8) heads of state invite heads of state from the developing world to attend some of their meetings. It would be desirable for the heads of state of developing countries to establish their own summit. There could be, for instance, a D–6 consisting of six developing democracies: Brazil, Mexico, India, Indonesia, Nigeria, and South Africa. The D–6 could then meet with the G–8 as equals, at least in appearance. This would be a first step toward reducing the disparity between center and periphery and establishing a more balanced world order.

The most important developing country is China. It is not a democracy, but it cannot be left out of any configuration that links together the developing world. The main obstacle to forming a D–6 is that the countries concerned do not want to offend China. China, in turn, has a real interest in making itself acceptable to the rest of the world. China is fast developing into a world power—and the longer it can continue developing without challenging other powers the better it is for its development. This strategy has been turned into a doctrine by the current leadership, which speaks of peaceful and harmonious development. At the same time, the power vacuum created by America's weakness is making China too powerful too fast for its own good. In its pursuit of energy supplies, it has become embroiled in a conflict with Japan, and it has become a rogue customer in Africa (e.g., Sudan) and Central Asia (e.g., Uzbekistan). It is important to link China closely into any emerging global architecture. That would help reinforce the doctrine of harmonious development and steer China in a constructive direction. China could be considered for membership in the G–8. In light of the recent autocratic tendencies in Russia, the G–8 can no longer be considered a group of democratic countries. If China were admitted, it would not mind being excluded from the D–6. The D–6, in turn, could cooperate more closely with the G–7 in promoting democracy, while meeting with the G–9 on economic issues.

INTERNATIONAL CIVIL SOCIETY

I believe there is great scope for civil society and NGOs to fill the leadership vacuum left by the disarray in the international community. Civil society cannot usurp the place occupied by sovereign states in a world order based on the principle of sovereignty, but democratic governments have to pay heed to the wishes of the people. Civil society can be effective by exerting influence on governments or, on specific issues, by working in association with governments.

Civil society has played an increasingly vociferous role in global affairs in recent years. The manifestations that captured the television screens involved riots directed against international organizations. It started with the Seattle riots in 1999 and continued at every gathering of the World Trade Organization, the World Bank and the International Monetary Fund, and the G–8. I consider these efforts sadly misdirected because they sought to gain publicity by creating unrest and by going after the wrong targets. The international institutions largely reflect the policies of the member states; it is the member states that have to be held responsible. Most of the misery and poverty in the world can be attributed to the policies of sovereign states; yet, they were not the targets of the demonstrations.

With less television coverage, civil society gave rise to two powerful forces, the human rights and environmental movements. They made both issues permanent features in national and international affairs. The Landmines Treaty and the ratification of the International Criminal Court were largely the work of international NGOs. More recently, a new movement is emerging that is directed against corruption in general and the resource curse in particular. It has the support of NGOs active in both movements, environmental and human rights. The corruption perception index published by Transparency International since 1995 has become well-known; the fight against the resource curse is more recent and has not yet entered into the awareness of the general public. Since I am intimately involved in it, I should like to draw attention to it.

The Resource Curse

Developing countries that are rich in natural resources tend to be just as poor as countries that are less well-endowed; what distinguishes them is that they usually have more repressive and corrupt governments and they are often wracked by armed conflicts. This has come to be known as the resource curse. The tale of the anti-resource curse movement is instructive because it is illustrative of what I call a fertile fallacy.

It all started with a campaign launched in early 2002 called Publish What You Pay. It was supported by a number of international NGOs, including Global Witness, which is grounded in the environmental movement and receives funding from my foundation.* The aim of the campaign was to persuade oil and mining companies to disclose all the payments they make to individual countries. The amounts could then be added together to establish how much each country receives. This would allow the citizens of those countries to hold their governments accountable for where the money goes. The name of the campaign was chosen by a publicity agent, and it turned out to be quite catchy. The campaign plugged into the prevailing sentiment against multinational corporations in the Western world, and it took off. The line of reasoning that led to the campaign, however, did not survive closer examination. (That is why I call it a fertile fallacy). Companies listed on the major stock exchanges could not be legally compelled to publish country-by-country accounts. When I discussed the matter with various supervisory

*Transparency International also received funding from us in its earlier days.

authorities, they told me that special legislation would be needed. The United States Congress with a Republican majority, for one, would never approve such legislation. And even if all publicly traded companies responded to public pressure, some important state owned and privately owned companies that do not raise funds on the major exchanges would remain exempt; as a result, the total amounts received by governments could not be accurately calculated. Consequently, I was eager to switch the attention of the movement from the companies to the governments.

Fortunately the British government, prompted by British NGOs, took the lead. The World Bank and the International Monetary Fund were also very supportive. With their help, the Extractive Industries Transparency Initiative (EITI) was born in late 2002; corporations, governments, and civil society were brought together to develop disclosure standards for companies and governments in oil-, gas-, and mining-dependent countries. EITI is not a catchy title, but with the backing of the British government and the Bretton Woods institutions it is gaining increasing international standing and support; more and more countries are expressing an interest in adhering to its transparency standards. Civil society provides the impetus to keep the initiative going. My foundation network is deeply involved. We have set up Revenue Watch groups in several countries to track payments to governments.

EITI works on a voluntary basis, but civil society continues to press for a compulsory approach. This keeps up the pressure on the oil and mining companies. British Petroleum did not need to be pushed. Its president, Lord John Browne, genuinely believes that greater transparency is in the interest of the shareholders, and he detailed British Petroleum's disbursements in Angola. The government of Angola threatened to cancel the company's concession on the grounds that it had violated the confidentiality clause which is a standard feature of international oil and gas contracts. British Petroleum had to back down in that case, but along with Shell, has announced that it will publish its payments in countries where the government allows it. Nigeria has waived the confidentiality clause and asked companies to report their payments individually. Other EITI adherents, including Azerbaijan, do not allow individual reporting, but ask all operating companies to pool their payment data for public reporting purposes. The civil society movement will continue to press for individual company disclosure, which offers greater transparency and accountability. Azerbaijan, where British Petroleum is the lead operator, has established an oil fund on the Norwegian model and adopted EITI principles. Kazakhstan has also set up an oil fund and has signed on to EITI. A dozen other countries have expressed an intention to adhere to EITI transparency principles.

The most dramatic advances were made in Nigeria, long a showcase for the resource curse, and its tiny neighbor Sao Tomé. President Olusegun Obasanjo had been associated with Transparency International before he returned to Nigeria and became president. After his reelection in 2003, with UNDP's financial support he brought back Ngozi Okonjo-Iweala from the World Bank and, assisted by a strong team of reformers,embarked on far-reaching fiscal, monetary, and banking reforms. Nigeria is a country in which practically everything has been tried but nothing ever worked; however, Ngozi, Oby Ezekwesili (the minister for solid minerals and driver of the Nigerian EITI process), Charles Soludo (governor of the Central Bank), and others have made major advances on institutional reform and transparency. The first independent forensic audits of oil revenues, production and management processes were recently published, pointing the way to further reforms in the oil and gas sector. With the help of my local foundation, the federal government also published its disbursements to the various state and local authorities. This led to some high-profile corruption prosecutions. Civil society, which had been very suspicious and hostile, began to believe in the process. The fiscal reforms also began to show results in the macroeconomic indicators. These developments helped Nigeria obtain substantial debt forgiveness as well as its first international credit rating.

The progress made in Nigeria is far from irreversible. Some of the richest and most powerful people feel endangered. People in the oil-producing regions see no benefits from the reforms so far. The efforts to halt corruption, piracy, and the stealing of oil have brought about a virtual insurrection in the Niger Delta. Presidential elections are due in 2007. There is no obvious successor to Obasanjo, and various regions are vying for the succession. Obasanjo is flirting with the idea of changing the country's constitution and standing for a third term. Until the succession is settled, the achievements of the last few years are at risk.

Sao Tomé is a small and impoverished island close to the coast of Nigeria whose off-shore oil fields are being developed in partnership with Nigeria. A group of lawyers acting pro bono provided technical assistance to help Sao Tomé adopt far-reaching transparency rules for its future oil and gas production. Advances are being made in many other parts of the world.

I am willing to back many initiatives, but I will keep backing them only if they generate their own momentum. The anti-resource curse initiative has stronger legs than most and that has made me very enthusiastic. In cooperation with the Hewlett foundation and other donors, we have decided to set up an independent organization, the Revenue Watch Institute, that will devise strategies, act as a theoretical and practical resource center, and provide technical assistance to those who ask for it. It is early days, but the outlook is promising. It is much easier to put existing resources to better use than to develop resources where they do not exist. As I like to put it, we have hit pay dirt.

The effort to cure the resource curse is a good example of what private foundations working with NGOs can accomplish. As I mentioned at the beginning of this section, civil society cannot replace sovereign states but it can influence how they, and other actors, such as multinational corporations, behave.

The main obstacle to further progress on the resource curse is China, and, to a lesser extent, India. In its quest for energy and other raw material supplies, China is fast becoming the sponsor of rogue regimes. It is the main trading partner and protector of the military dictatorship in Myanmar. It feted President Islam Karimov of Uzbekistan immediately after the massacre at Andijan, and it conferred an honorary degree on President Robert Mugabe of Zimbabwe. It is the main buyer of Sudan's oil, and it hindered the work of the United Nations in dealing with ethnic cleansing in Darfur. It extended a large credit to Angola when Angola failed to meet the conditions imposed by the International Monetary Fund. China's behavior poses an obstacle that civil society cannot overcome on its own. Civil society can exert pressure on the multinationals, but not on China or India. The energy policy pursued by these countries will require the attention of governments. I shall elaborate this point in the next chapter.

CHAPTER 7

The Global Energy Crisis

A common theme connects many of the issues discussed in the second part of the book. Let me pull the various threads together: global warming, the resource curse, the increasing energy dependence of the major economies—the United States, Europe, Japan, China, and India—on politically unstable countries and regions, the tight supply situation, the increasing instability of the Middle East. It adds up to a major crisis facing humanity: a global energy crisis.

The various components have been slowly maturing over a long period of time. The global warming we are currently experiencing has been caused by emissions of greenhouse gases that started more than a century ago. The resource curse has its origins in colonial times and is a major contributor to the instability of the Middle East. Oil production in the United States peaked decades ago, in 1971; a theory called Hubbert's Peak holds that global oil production is about to do the same. According to this theory, we are very close to the peak, but it would be too much of a coincidence if it were to happen right now.

All the various components came together after 9/11, and

9/11 was a major factor in bringing them together. Once we realize this, many other developments discussed in the book fall into place: the war on terror; the invasion of Iraq; the rise of Iran; the radicalization of Islam and the increasing sectarian tensions within Islam; the decline in American power and influence; nuclear proliferation; China's pursuit of natural resources and its negative effect on curing the resource curse; and Russia's use of gas supplies to suborn its former empire and the danger that it poses for Europe.

The core of the crisis is the tight supply situation for oil. The reasons are partly secular and partly cyclical. The secular factor is that oil consumption regularly exceeds the discovery of new reserves. In 2004, 30 billion barrels were consumed, but only 8 billion barrels were discovered. Excess capacity has fallen from 12 million barrels per day in 1988 to fewer than 2 million barrels per day currently. An American geophysicist, M. King Hubbert, constructed a theoretical model of oil availability (Hubbert's Peak), and based on that model he predicted in 1956 that United States oil production would peak between 1965 and 1970; in 1971, he predicted that global oil production would peak between 1995 and 2000. Since he was so close to being right about the United States, his many followers predict that global production has peaked or will peak very soon. The controversy that surrounds these predictions is largely beside the point; the peak can be delayed for a while by using more aggressive and expensive extraction methods. The point is that when a field is half depleted, it becomes increasingly difficult to extract the remaining oil. Most of the giant fields are past the halfway mark, and no new giant field has been found anywhere since 1951, when one was found in Saudi Arabia.* Depletion figures are notoriously unreliable, but the available evidence indicates that they have been understated. Many publicly traded companies had to restate their reserves downwards, and many of the established producing countries report declining production. The country enjoying the biggest potential reserves, Saudi Arabia, does not provide figures on the depletion of existing fields.

Although the secular trend is clear, most of the near-term fluctuations are due to cyclical factors. Demand has been strong, partly because of the strength of the global economy and partly because of the rise of China, India, and other developing countries which are less energy-efficient than the mature economies. In addition to the tightness in crude supplies, there is a shortage of refining capacity. The fastest-growing demand is for middle distillates (diesel, jet fuel, and heating oil); but most of the new supplies are heavy crudes, which are difficult to refine into these products. Natural gas supplies are much further away from peaking, but there is a shortage of transportation. These shortages will be overcome in due course. Indeed, the temporary tightness will almost unavoidably be followed by a temporary glut. Right now, the consuming countries believe that they do not have enough inventory. That, together with speculative positions, boosts demand. When supply catches up, these two sources of demand will drop. The tight supply situation has created an incentive to interfere with supplies for political purposes,

*Giant field is defined as 30 billion barrels plus. See Roger D. Blanchard, *The Future of Global Oil Production* (Jefferson, North Carolina: McFarland & Co., Inc., 2005). Also see Matthew R. Simmons, *Twilight in the Desert—The Coming Saudi Oil Shock and the World Economy* (Hoboken, NJ: John Wiley & Sons Inc., 2005).

as has happened in Nigeria and could happen in Venezuela and Iran. When the bottlenecks are removed, the incentive to interfere with supplies is reduced. All these factors will combine to depress prices. OPEC will arrest the decline by restricting output, thereby creating the excess capacity that is needed to forestall supply interruptions. But the other elements of the global energy crisis—global warming, dependence on politically unstable areas, the resource curse, and eventually Hubbert's Peak—will remain. The temporary glut may sap the political will to deal with them; indeed, that is what happened after the first energy crisis in the 1970s. It is liable to happen again.

The global energy crisis poses a threat in many ways, though some of the connections are difficult to see. Global warming has little to do with terrorism or with the success of President Hugo Chavez in Venezuela. Yet these disparate developments are connected by the global energy crisis and recognizing the connections helps to put the present moment into a new perspective. For instance, Vice President Dick Cheney used to frighten people by suggesting that terrorists might obtain weapons of mass destruction, and Democrats are still trying to score points by stressing the security of our ports. The real threat is terrorists and others—pirates in Nigeria, Hugo Chavez in Venezuela, and al Qaeda in the Middle East—might disrupt the energy supply chain. This threat was made real on February 24, 2006, when terrorists penetrated the outer gate of the Abqaiq facility in Saudi Arabia—which is capable of processing approximately 10 percent of global energy supply—but were stopped by members of the National Guard. Even though the attack did not have an immediate impact on Saudi oil supplies, it signified an attempt to target the oil infrastructure, a departure from prior tactics.

The various elements in the global energy crisis are easier to tackle when the connections are recognized than they would be on their own. Take one example: deriving a carbon-free fuel from coal. If an efficient technology were developed it could make a major contribution to reducing carbon emissions; it would also reduce the dependence of the United States and China, which have enormous coal reserves, on imported energy; and, of course, it would be an antidote to Hubbert's Peak. Any one of these considerations may not be sufficient to generate support for carbon extraction from coal, but the three taken together ought to make it a top priority. But carbon extraction also requires energy and current technologies are not fuel-efficient enough; substantial investments in new technologies will be required.

No single measure is sufficient to ease the crisis. Many different actions will have to be taken at the same time, in addition to carbon-free coal, nuclear energy, wind, biomass, and, of course, demand reduction. That is where the price mechanism can be useful: A carbon tax combined with carbon credits would provide the economic incentives to introduce the appropriate adjustments both on the demand side and on the supply side. The Kyoto Protocol set targets for carbon emissions and facilitated the trading of carbon credits. It was a step in the right direction, but it did not go far enough.

The global energy crisis is more complex than any other crisis. It is not a single crisis but a confluence of disparate developments that have reinforced each other and reached crisis point more or less at the same time. They endanger our civilization in various ways. Global warming and nuclear proliferation have already been discussed. But they are only aspects of a more complex situation that threatens to deteriorate into global disintegration. Although the core of the crisis is the tight supply situation for oil, the developments that may bring about disintegration are mainly political.

The global energy crisis may be interpreted as the flip side of globalization. The extent to which it endangers our civilization depends on how we deal with it. Our civilization has survived many crises. Financial markets often go to the brink and then recoil. Only rarely do they go over the brink, as they did in the Asian crisis of 1997. Even then, the authorities intervened when the center of the global financial system came under threat. That is why it is now described as the Asian crisis and did not become a full-fledged crisis of global capitalism. Our political system is less well-equipped to avoid disaster. We have experienced two world wars and we have had some close brushes with a third one. Wars have a tendency to become increasingly devastating. The threat of nuclear war should not be minimized. Our civilization is fuelled by energy; the global energy crisis could destroy it.

The magnitude and multitude of the problems exceed our capacity to deal with them, or even to comprehend them. The present acute phase of the crisis is the outgrowth of misconceptions, particularly those related to 9/11. Although we cannot rid ourselves of misconceptions, we can correct them when we become aware of them. Perhaps the biggest mistake is for the United States to think that it is powerful enough to deal with these problems on its own. The competitive position of one state vis-à-vis the others is not what matters when the viability and sustainability of the world order is at stake. Our definition of national security is too narrow, and the prevailing view that the world order, like a market, will take care of itself if left alone, is plain wrong. Global warming, energy dependency, the resource curse, and the nuclear non-proliferation regime require international cooperation.

Although the global energy crisis demands international cooperation, we must be wary of going to the opposite extreme and disregarding the national interests of sovereign states. No matter what systemic changes are introduced, they need to take these interests into account. Consider China. Until 1993, it was self-sufficient in oil; now it imports almost half its consumption. Its share of the world oil market is only 8 percent, but it accounts for 30 percent of incremental demand. China has a genuine interest in harmonious development. It also has a serious energy-dependence problem as well as serious pollution problems. Therefore, it is a natural partner for developing alternative clean fuels, particularly from coal, which is plentiful in China. But China is not a natural partner in curing the resource curse. On the contrary, in its search for alternative energy sources it has become a customer of rogue states in Africa and Central Asia, a situation that is contrary to China's interest in harmonious development; but its leadership sees no alternative, particularly after its bid for Unocal was rebuffed. It would behoove the United States government to allow China to acquire stakes in legitimate energy companies, but *only* if it cooperated in dealing with the resource curse.

Europe ought to lead the way in energy cooperation. It is heavily dependent on natural gas and Russia is its main supplier. The European Union imports 50 percent of its energy needs, and imports are projected to rise to 70 percent by 2020. Russia is by far the biggest supplier of its imported oil

(20 percent) and natural gas (40 percent). Many EU countries depend heavily on gas from Russia, which supplies 40 percent of Germany's total demand, 65–80 percent of Poland's, Hungary's, and the Czech Republic's demand, and almost 100 percent of the gas needs of Austria, Slovakia, and the Baltic states. This makes Europe particularly vulnerable because Russia has begun to use its control over gas supplies as a political weapon. The story is a complicated one and I can give only a brief outline here. When the Soviet system disintegrated, the energy sector was privatized in a chaotic fashion. Devious transactions were perpetrated, like the loan for shares scheme, and enormous fortunes were made. When Vladimir Putin became president, he used the power of the state to regain control of the energy industry. He put the president of Yukos, Mikhail Khodorkovsky, in jail and bankrupted the company. He put his own man, Alexey Miller, in charge of Gazprom and pushed out the previous management that had built a private fiefdom out of Gazprom's properties. But he did not dissolve the fiefdom but used it to assert control over the production and transportation of gas in the neighboring countries. This led to the formation of a network of shady companies that served the dual purpose of extending Russian influence and creating private wealth. Billions of dollars were siphoned off over the years. The most valuable asset was the gas of Turkmenistan which was resold by a company registered in Hungary at a multiple of the price at which it was bought. While the ownership of Eural Trans Gas was never disclosed, the decisions to give it contracts were made jointly by President Putin and the then-president of Ukraine, Leonid Kuchma. I believe that was one of the reasons why Putin exposed himself so pub-

licly in backing Kuchma's nominee, Viktor Yanukovich, for president of Ukraine in 2004. After the Orange Revolution, the contract with Turkmenistan passed into the hands of RosUkrEnergo, a company with shady ownership set up by Raiffeisenbank of Austria. At the beginning of 2006, Russia cut off the gas supply to Ukraine. Ukraine, in turn, tapped into the gas that was passing through Ukraine on its way to Europe. This forced Russia to restore supplies to Ukraine; but in the subsequent settlement, Russia gained the upper hand: It promised gas supplies at reduced prices through RosUkrEnergo for six months, but Ukraine committed itself to fixing the transit fees for five years. After six months, Russia will be able to exert political pressure on Ukraine by threatening to raise gas prices. Russia already exercises control over Belarus.

The net result is that Europe is relying for a large portion of its energy supplies on a country that does not hesitate to use its monopoly power in arbitrary ways. Until now, European countries have been competing with each other to obtain supplies from Russia. This has put them at Russia's mercy. Energy dependence is having a major influence on the attitude and policies of the European Union towards Russia and its neighbors. It will serve the national interests of the member states to develop a European energy policy. Acting together, they can improve the balance of power. In the short run, Russia is in the driver's seat; An interruption of gas supplies disrupts European economies immediately while an interruption of gas revenues would affect Russia only with a delay. In the long run, the situation is reversed. Russia needs a market for its gas and few alternatives exist as long as Europe sticks together. Europe could use its bargaining

power by telling Russia that under present conditions its dependence on Russian gas is excessive. If Russia wants to
maintain and increase its market in Europe, it must agree to a
change in conditions by signing the European Energy Charter
and the Extractive Industries Transparency Initiative. This
would break up the Russian gas monopoly, turn the pipelines
into highways and allow Europe to increase its gas imports
from the former Soviet Union without endangering its energy security. The European Union has its origin in the Coal
and Steel Community; it could regain political momentum
by developing an effective common energy policy.

Meanwhile, encouraged by the energy shortage and
America's weakness, Russia is assuming an increasingly assertive posture that goes well beyond energy policy. Russia
has sold Iran Tor and (through Belarus) S300 anti-aircraft
missiles and has refused to rescind the sale in spite of strong
U.S. pressure. The missiles will be installed by the fall of
2006 and after that time it will be more difficult for Israel to
deliver a preemptive strike against the Iranian nuclear installations.* Russia has also granted Hamas a $10 million-a-
month subsidy to replace the subsidy withdrawn by the
European Union and is reported to be selling arms to
Syria.†

These decisions mean that Russia is reasserting itself as a
major player in the Middle East, playing against Western interests. Underlying all this is a shift in Russia's national security
doctrine which has been publicly announced but has re-

*Andrei Piontkovsky, "Putin's Plan for Conflict with Iran", *The Jerusalem Post*,
February 1, 2006.
†http://abcnews.go.com/International/wireStory?id=710975; http://www.mosnews.
com/news/2005/02/10/armstrade.shtml; http://news.monstersandcritics.com/
mcreports/article_1130746.php/Russian_arms_sales_to_the_Middle_East_.

ceived little attention.* Evidence is accumulating that Russia may be deliberately promoting an Israeli missile attack on Iran by supplying missile defense to Iran and launching a satellite for Israel that will be used to monitor Iran's nuclear activities.†

It is difficult to present a well-considered assessment of the situation because events are unfolding rapidly even as these lines are written (May 2006). All I can do is mention some of the threads that need to be woven together. First, the resource curse: The peculiar dynamic that prevails in countries whose economies depend primarily on revenues from natural resources. Second, the history of Russia since the collapse of the Soviet Union: the chaotic conditions, the wide-spread misery combined with the incredible wealth and success of a few adventurers, the humiliation suffered by Russia as a superpower—far greater than the humiliation of Germany after the First World War. Third: the emergence of a new leadership in Russia that has its roots in the KGB but whose world view has been shaped by the far-from-equilibrium conditions which have prevailed since the Soviet Union collapsed. Fourth: the threat posed by the so-called color revolutions in Georgia, Ukraine, and Kyrgyzstan. Fifth: turmoil in the Middle East, the energy shortage, and the precipitous decline of the remaining superpower, the United States.

Trying to weave these threads together, the pattern that seems to be emerging is a shocking one: an adventurous

*Sergei Ivanov, "Russia Must be Strong," *The Wall Street Journal*, January 11, 2006; and Sergei Lavrov, "Russia in Global Affairs," *Moscow News*, March 10, 2006.
†"Russia Helps Israel Keep an Eye on Iran," *The New York Times*, April 25, 2006 (Moscow: Associated Press).

regime in Russia (very different from the stodgy, cautious, and conservative leadership of the Soviet Union) that sees an opportunity to consolidate its power and acquire immense wealth and power based on natural resources. Russia seems to be emerging as a new kind of player on the international scene, a petro-superpower that needs to foment conflict in the Middle East in order to fulfill its aspirations.

I am astounded by this possibility. Although I follow developments in Russia fairly closely, I have been taken unawares. In this respect I am no different from the rest of the world. We are so preoccupied with our internal disagreements that we fail to see gathering external threats. We are still fighting a phantasmagorical war on terror while a real conflagration is looming.

President Bush has reaffirmed his intention to attend the G8 meeting in St. Petersburg in July 2006, in spite of Russia's refusal to stop missile sales to Iran. He intends to use Russia as an intermediary for getting concessions from Iran just as we are using China as an intermediary with North Korea. But this is a false track. The United States needs to negotiate with Iran directly. Russia has its own agenda. The Putin regime craves the respectability that the G8 meeting in St. Petersburg would confer. The regime will have greater latitude in pursuing an independent line afterward. In retrospect, unless the missile sales to Iran are stopped, Bush's attendance in St. Petersburg may well come to resemble Neville Chamberlin going to Munich. Russia seems to be counting on the disunity and inertia of the West. Unfortunately, its calculation may prove to be correct. Both the United States and Europe are internally divided and far apart from each other; the European Union is held together by bureaucratic inertia. The business community is also inclined to seek individual deals with Russia rather than to demand certain standards of behavior. There is an urgent need for the West to pull together.

International cooperation ought to extend beyond the immediate emergency. Global warming requires a global solution, but the attitude of the Bush administration stands in the way. On this issue, the American public is ahead of the administration, and it ought to impose its views on the government.

The most pressing task is to agree upon a new non-proliferation treaty. The present treaty is breaking down. Iran is determined to develop its nuclear capabilities and if it is not stopped, nothing can stop a number of other countries from doing the same thing. A missile attack on Iran in the current circumstances would be counter-productive. It would consolidate public support for the current regime and reinforce the determination of the regime to develop nuclear bombs. It would unite the Moslem and much of the developing world against the United States. It would render the position of the occupying forces in Iraq untenable and it would disrupt the world economy without stopping Iran from eventually having nuclear bombs. Both scenarios lead to disaster. The only way out is to agree upon a more equitable non-proliferation regime that would have near universal support. Iran would either agree to join such a regime or it could be forced to do so without incurring the disastrous consequences that a missile attack under the current circumstances would entail.

The global energy crisis, and all it implies, is a major challenge confronting our globalized civilization. It ought to be sufficient to bring about a change of attitude in the United States, provide a focal point for the cohesion of the European Union, and put some content into the concept of a global open society. It will certainly provide a focal point for my future involvement and for the future activities of my foundations. We are already at the cutting edge of fighting the resource curse; we are getting involved in global warming; we intend to take a more active interest in the future of the European Union; and I personally will continue to plead for a fundamental rethinking of America's role in the world.

Appendix:
The Original Framework

The conceptual framework presented here formed part of an unpublished manuscript entitled *The Burden of Consciousness* written in 1963. I revised it slightly for inclusion in my 1990 book, *Opening The Soviet System*. Since that book was published in 1300 copies of which I bought 1000, I felt it was worth including it again in this book.

THE CONCEPT OF CHANGE

Change is an abstraction. It does not exist by itself but is always combined with a substance that is changing or is subject to change. Of course, the substance in question is also an abstraction, without independent existence. The only thing that really exists is substance-cum-change, which is separated into substance and change by the human mind in its quest to introduce some sense into a confusing universe. Here we are not concerned with changes as they occur in reality, but with change as a concept.

The important point about change as a concept is that it requires abstract thinking. Awareness of change is associated with a mode of thinking which is characterized by the use of abstractions; lack of awareness involves the lack of abstractions. We can construct two distinct modes of thinking along those lines.

In the absence of change the mind has to deal only with one set of circumstances: that which exists at the present time. What has gone before and what will come in the future is identical with what exists now. Past, present and future form a unity, and the whole range of possibilities is reduced to one concrete case: things are as they are because they could not be any other way. This principle simplifies the task of thinking tremendously; the mind needs to operate only with concrete information, and all the complications arising out of the use of abstractions can be avoided. I shall call this the traditional mode of thinking.

Now let us consider a changing world. Man must learn to think not only of things as they are but also as they have been and as they could be. There is then not only the present to consider but an infinite range of possibilities. How can they be reduced to manageable proportions? Only by introducing generalizations, dichotomies, and other abstractions. Once it comes to generalizations, the more general they are, the more they simplify matters. This world is best conceived as a general equation in which the present is represented by one set of constants. Change the constants and the same equation will apply to all past and future situations. Working with general equations of this kind, one must be prepared to accept any set of constants which conforms to them. In other words, everything is to be considered possible, unless it has proven to be impossible. I shall call this the critical mode of thinking.

The traditional and critical modes of thinking are based on two diametrically opposed principles. Yet they each present an internally consistent view of reality. How is that possible? Only by presenting a distorted view. But the distortion need not be as great as it would be if it applied to the same set of circumstances because, in accordance with the theory of reflexivity, the circumstances are bound to be influenced by the prevailing mode of thinking. The traditional mode of thinking is associated with what I shall call organic society, the critical mode with "open" society. This provides the starting point for the theoretical models I seek to establish.

How closely a prevailing form of society needs to conform to the prevailing mode of thinking will be one of the questions we must ask in building the models. Even if social conditions are susceptible to the participants' thinking, there are other aspects of reality which are not so easily influenced. Nature is particularly obdurate in this respect: It fails to obey people's wishes as people have discovered in the course of history. Each mode of thinking must therefore have a mechanism for dealing with phenomena that do not conform to its concept of change. That will be another issue to consider. Most importantly, each model must have a flaw which is apparent to us even if it is not apparent to the participants.

The Traditional Mode of Thinking

Things are as they have always been—therefore they could not be any other way. This may be taken as the central tenet of the traditional mode of thinking. Its logic is less than perfect; indeed, it contains the built-in-flaw we expect to find in our models. The fact that its central tenet is neither true nor logical reveals an important feature of the traditional mode of thinking: it is neither so critical nor so logical as we have learned to be. It does not need to be. Logic and other forms of argument are useful only when one has to choose between alternatives.

Changeless society is characterized by the absence of alternatives. There is only one set of circumstances the human mind has to deal with: they way things are. While alternatives can be imagined, they appear like fairy tales because the path that would lead to them is missing.

In such circumstances, the proper attitude is to accept things as they seem to be. The scope for speculation and criticism is limited: the primary task of thinking is not to question but to come to terms with a given situation—a task that can be performed without any but the most pedestrian kind of generalizations. This saves people a great deal of trouble. At the same time, it deprives them of the more elaborate tools of critical thinking. Their view of the world is bound to be primitive and distorted.

Both the advantages and the drawbacks become apparent when we consider the problems of epistemology. The relationship of thoughts to reality does not arise as a problem. There is no world of ideas separate from the world of facts; and, even more important, there seems to be nothing subjective or personal about thinking: it is firmly rooted in the tradition handed down by generations; its validity is beyond question. Prevailing ideas are accepted as reality itself, or, to be more precise, the distinction between ideas and reality is simply not drawn.

This may be demonstrated by looking at the way language is used. Naming something is like attaching a label to it. When we think in concrete terms, there is always a "thing" to which a name corresponds and we can use the name and the thing interchangeably: thinking and reality are co-extensive. Only if we think in abstract terms do we begin giving names to things which do not exist independently of our naming them. We may be under the impression that we are still attaching labels to "things" yet these "things" have only come into existence through our labeling them; the labels are attached to something that was created in our mind. This is the point at which thinking and reality become separated.

By confining itself to concrete terms, the traditional mode of thinking avoids the separation. But it has to pay heavily for this supreme simplicity. If no distinction is made between thinking and reality, how can one distinguish between true and false? The only statement that can be rejected is one that does not conform to the prevailing tradition. Traditional views must automatically be accepted because there is no criterion for rejecting them. The way things appear is the way things are: the traditional mode of thinking cannot probe any deeper. It cannot establish causal relationships between various occurrences because these could prove to be either true or false; if they were false there would be a reality apart from our thinking, and the very foundations of the traditional mode of thinking would be undermined. Yet if thinking and reality are to be regarded as identical, an explanation must be provided for everything. The existence of a question without an answer would destroy the unity of thinking and reality just as surely as would the existence of a right and wrong answer.

Fortunately it is possible to explain the world without recourse to causal laws. Everything behaves according to its nature. Since there is no distinction between natural and supernatural, all questions can be put to rest by endowing objects with a spirit whose influence explains any occurrence whatsoever and eliminates the possibility of internal contradictions. Most objects will seem to be under the command of such a force because in the absence of causal laws most behavior has an arbitrary quality about it.

When the distinction between thoughts and reality is missing, an explanation carries the same conviction whether it is based on observation or irrational belief. The spirit of a tree enjoys the same kind of existence as its body, provided we believe in it. Nor do we have reason to doubt our beliefs: our forefathers believed in the same thing. In this way the traditional mode of thinking with its simple epistemology may easily lead to beliefs that are completely divorced from reality.

To believe in spirits and their magic is equivalent to accepting our surroundings as being beyond our control. This attitude is profoundly appropriate to a changeless society. Since people are powerless to change the world in which they live, their task is to acquiesce in their fate. By humbly accepting the authority of the spirits who rule the world, they may propitiate them; but to probe into the secrets of the universe will not do any good at all. Even if they did discover the causes of certain phenomena, the knowledge would bring no practical advantage unless they believed that they could change the conditions of their existence, which is unthinkable. The only motive for enquiry that remains is idle curiosity; and whatever inclination they may have to indulge in it, the danger of angering the spirits will effectively discourage it. Thus the search for causal explanations is likely to be absent from people's thoughts.

In a changeless society social conditions are indistinguishable from natural phenomena. They are determined by tradition and it is just as much beyond the power of people to change then as it is to change the rest of their surroundings. The distinction between social and natural laws is one that the traditional mode of thinking is incapable of recognizing. Hence the same attitude of humble submissiveness is required towards society as towards nature.

We have seen that the traditional mode of thinking fails to distinguish between thoughts and reality, truth and falsehood, social and natural laws. If we searched further, other omissions could be found. For instance, the traditional mode of thinking is very vague on the question of time: past, present and future tend to melt into each other. Such categories are indispensable to us. Judging the traditional mode of thinking from our vantage point, we find it quite inadequate. It is not so, however, in the conditions in which it prevails. In a really changeless society it fulfills its function perfectly: it contains all necessary concrete information while avoiding unnecessary complications. It represents the simplest possible way of dealing with the simplest possible world. Its major weakness is not its lack of subtlety but the fact that the concrete information it contains is inferior to that which can be attained by a different approach. This is obvious to us, blessed as we are with superior knowledge. It need not disturb those who have no knowledge other than tradition; but it does make the whole structure extremely vulnerable to outside influences. A rival system of thought can destroy the monopolistic position of existing beliefs and force them to be subjected to critical examination. This would mean the end of the traditional mode of thinking and the beginning of the critical mode.

Take the case with medicine. The tribal medicine man has a completely false picture of the workings of the human body. Long experience has taught him the usefulness of certain treatments but he is liable to do the right things for the wrong reasons. Nevertheless he is regarded with awe by the tribe; his failures are attributed to the evil spirits with whom he is on familiar terms but for whose actions he is not responsible. Only when modern medical science comes into direct competition with primitive medicine does the superiority of correct explanations over mistaken ones become manifest. However grudgingly and suspiciously, the tribe is eventually forced to accept the white man's medicine because it works better.

The traditional mode of thinking can also come up against difficulties of its own making. As we have seen, at least part of the prevailing body of beliefs is bound to be false. Even in a simple and unchanging society, some unusual events occur which must be accounted for. The new explanation may contradict the established one, and the struggle between them might tear apart the wonderfully simple structure of the traditional world. Yet the traditional mode of thinking need not break down every time there is a change in the conditions of existence. Tradition is extremely flexible as long as it is not threatened by alternatives. It encompasses all prevailing explanations by definition. As soon as a new explanation prevails, it automatically becomes the traditional one and, with the distinction between past and present blurred, it will seem to have prevailed since timeless times. In this way, even a changing world may appear to be changeless within fairly wide limits.

It can be seen therefore that in a simple and relatively unchanging world the traditional mode of thinking may satisfy the needs of people indefinitely, but if they are exposed to alien ways of thinking or if new developments create a more complex situation, it is liable to break down.

Traditional beliefs may be able to retain their supremacy in competition with other ideas, especially if they are supported by the requisite amount of coercion. Under these circumstances, however, the mode of thinking can no longer be regarded as traditional. It is not the same to declare the principle that things must be as they always have been as to believe in it implicitly. In order to uphold such a principle, one view must be upheld as correct and all others eliminated. Tradition may serve as the touchstone of what is eligible and what is not; but it can no longer be what it was for the traditional mode of thinking, the sole source of knowledge. To distinguish the pseudo-traditional from the original, I refer to it as the "dogmatic mode of thinking" and I shall discuss it separately.

ORGANIC SOCIETY

The traditional mode of thinking does not recognize the distinction between social and natural laws: the social framework is considered just as unalterable as the rest of man's environment. Hence the starting point in a changeless society is always the social Whole and not the individuals who comprise it. While society fully determines the existence of its members, the members have no say in determining the nature of the society in which they live because that has been fixed for them by tradition. This does not mean that there is a conflict of interest between the individual and the Whole in which the individual must always lose out. In a changeless society the individual as such does not exist at all: moreover, the social Whole is not an abstract idea which stands in contrast to the idea of the individual but a concrete unity that embraces all members. The dichotomy between the social Whole and the individual, like so many others, is the result of our habit of using abstract terms. In order to understand the unity that characterizes a changeless society, we must discard some of our ingrained habits of thought, and especially our concept of the individual.

The individual is an abstract concept and as such it has no place in a changeless society. Society has members, each of whom is capable of thinking and feeling: but, instead of being fundamentally similar, they are fundamentally different according to their station in life. It would not even occur or them that they are in some way equal.

Just as the individual as an abstraction has no existence, so the social Whole exists not as an abstraction but as a concrete fact. The unity of a changeless society is comparable to the unity of an organism. Members of a changeless society are like organs of a body. They cannot live outside of society, and within it there is only one position available to them: that which they occupy. The functions they fulfill to determine their rights and duties. A peasant differs from a priest as greatly as the stomach from the brain. It is true that people have the ability to think and feel, but as their position in society is fixed, the net effect is not very different than if they had no consciousness at all.

The analogy applies only as long as the members accept their assigned role unquestionably. Paradoxically, the analogy is usually put forward when the traditional framework of society is already threatened: people living in a truly changeless society would have neither the need nor the ability to think of it. The fact that Menenius Agrippa found it necessary to propose the analogy indicates that the established order was in trouble. The term "organic society" only applies to a society in which the analogy would never be thought of, and it becomes false the moment it is used.

The unity of an organic society is anathema to another kind of unity, that of mankind. Since the traditional mode of thinking employs no abstract concepts, every relationship is concrete and particular. The fundamental similarity of one man to another and the inalienable rights of man are ideas of another age. The mere fact of being human has no rights attached to it: a slave is no different from another chattel in the eyes of the law. For instance, in a feudal society the land is more important that the landlord; the latter derives his privileges only by virtue of the land he holds.

Rights and titles may be hereditary, but this does not turn then into private property. We may be inclined to consider private property as something very concrete; actually it is the opposite. To separate a relationship into rights and duties is already an abstraction; in its concrete form it implies both. The concept of private property goes even further; it implies absolute possession without any obligations. As such, it is diametrically opposed to the principle of organic society, in which every possession carries corresponding obligations.

Nor does organic society recognize justice as an abstract principle. Justice exists only as a collection of concrete rights and obligations. Nevertheless, the administration of law involves a certain kind of generalization. Except in a society that is so changeless as to be dead, each case differs in some precedent in order to make it applicable. Without abstract principles to guide him, it depends upon the judge how he performs his task. There is at least a chance that the new decision will be in conflict with the precedent in some respect. Fortunately this need not cause any difficulties since the new ruling itself immediately becomes a precedent that can guide later decisions.

What emerges from such a process is common law, as opposed to legislative statutes. It is based on the unspoken assumption that the decisions of the past continue to apply indefinitely. The assumption is strictly speaking false but it is so useful that it may continue to prevail long after society has ceased to be organic. The effective administration of justice requires that the rules be known in advance. In view of man's imperfect knowledge, legislation cannot foresee all contingencies, and precedents are necessary to supplement the statutes. Common law can function side by side with statute law because, in spite of the underlying assumption of changelessness, it can imperceptibly adjust itself to changing circumstances. By the same token organic society could not survive the codification of its laws because it would lose its flexibility. Once laws are codified the appearance of changelessness cannot be maintained and organic society disintegrates. Fortunately, the need to codify laws, draw up contracts, or record tradition in any permanent way is not very pressing as long as tradition is not threatened by alternatives.

The unity of organic society means that its members have no choice but to belong to it. It goes even further. It implies that they have no desire but to belong to it, for their interests and those of society are the same: they indemnify themselves with society. Unity is not a principle proclaimed by the authorities but a fact accepted by all participants. No great sacrifice is involved. One's place in society may be onerous or undignified but it is the only one available; without it, one has no place in the world.

Nevertheless, there are bound to be people who do not abide by the prevailing mode of thinking. How society deals with such people is the supreme test of its adaptability. Repression is bound to be counterproductive because it provokes conflict and may encourage the evolution of an alternative way of thinking. Tolerance mixed with disbelief is probably the most effective answer. Craziness and madness in all its variety can be particularly useful in dealing with people who think differently and primitive societies are noted for their tolerance of the mentally afflicted.

It is only when traditional ties are sufficiently loosened to enable people to change their relative positions within society by their own efforts that they come to dissociate their own interests from those of the Whole. When this happens, the unity of organic society falls apart and everyone seeks to pursue his self-interest. Traditional relationships may be preserved in such circumstances, too, but only by coercion. That is no longer a truly organic society but one that is kept artificially changeless. The distinction is the same as that between the traditional and dogmatic modes of thinking and to emphasize it I shall refer to this state of affairs as closed society.

THE CRITICAL MODE OF THINKING

Abstractions

As long as people believe that the world is changeless, they can rest happily in the conviction that their view of the world is the only conceivable one. Tradition, however far removed from reality, provides guidance and thinking need never move beyond the consideration of concrete situations.

In a changing world, however, the present does not slavishly repeat the past. Instead of a course fixed by tradition, people are confronted by an infinite range of possibilities. To introduce some order into an otherwise confusing universe they are obliged to resort to simplifications, generalizations, abstractions, causal laws and all kinds of other mental aids.

Thought processes do not only help solve problems; they create their own. Abstractions open reality to different interpretations. Since they are only aspects of reality, one interpretation does not exclude all others: every situation has as many aspects as the mind discovers in it. If this feature of abstract thinking were fully understood, abstractions would create fewer problems. People would realize that they are dealing with a simplified image of the situation and not the situation itself. But even if everyone were fully versed in the intricacies of modern linguistic philosophy the problems would not disappear because abstractions play a dual role. In relation to the things they describe they represent aspects of reality without having a concrete existence themselves. For instance, the law of gravity does not make apples fall to the ground but merely explains the forces that do. In relation to the people who employ them, however, abstractions are very much a part of reality: by influencing attitudes and actions they have a major impact on events. For instance, the discovery of the law of gravity changed people's behavior. In so far as people think about their own situation, it becomes reflexive. Instead of a clear-cut separation between thoughts and reality, the infinite variety of a changing world is compounded by the infinite variety of interpretation that abstract thinking can produce.

Abstract thinking tends to create categories which contrast opposite aspects of the real world against each other. Time and Space; Society and the Individual; Material and the Ideal are typical dichotomies of this kind. Needless to say, the models I am constructing here also belong to the collection. These categories are no more real than the abstractions that gave rise to them. That is to say, they represent a simplification or distortion of reality in the first place but, through their influence on people's thinking, they may also introduce divisions and conflicts into the real world. They contribute to making reality more complex and abstractions more necessary. In this way the process of abstraction feeds on itself: the complexities of a changing world are, to a large extent, of man's own making.

In view of the complications, why do people employ abstract concepts at all? The answer is that they avoid them as much as possible. As long as the world can be regarded as changeless, they use no abstractions at all. Even when abstractions become indispensable, they prefer to treat them as part of reality rather than as the product of their own thinking. Only bitter experience will teach them to distinguish between their own thoughts and reality. The tendency to neglect the complications connected with the use of abstractions must be regarded as a weakness of the critical mode of thinking because abstraction are indispensable to it, and the less they are understood the greater confusion they create.

Despite their drawbacks, abstractions serve us well. It is true that they create new problems, but the mind responds to these with renewed efforts until thinking reaches degrees of intricacy and refinement which would be unimaginable in the traditional mode. A changing world does not lend itself to the kind of certainty that would be readily available if society were changeless, but in its less than perfect way of thinking can provide much valuable knowledge. Abstractions generate an infinite variety of views; as long as a fairly effective method is available for choosing between them, the critical mode should be able to come much closer to reality that the traditional mode which has only one interpretation at its disposal.

THE CRITICAL PROCESS

Choosing between alternatives may then be regarded as the key function of the critical mode of thinking. People cannot commit themselves to a particular view without at least being aware of the alternatives and rejecting them for one reason or another. The traditional mode of thinking accepts explanations uncritically, but, in a changing society, no one can say "this is how things are, therefore they cannot be any other way." People must support their views with arguments, otherwise they will convince no one but themselves; and to believe unconditionally in an idea rejected by everyone else is a form of madness. Even those who believe they have the final answer must take into account possible objections and defend themselves against criticism.

The critical mode of thinking is more than an attitude: it is a prevailing condition. It denotes a situation in which there are a large number of divergent interpretations; their proponents seek to gain acceptance for the ideas in which they believe. If the traditional mode of thinking represents an intellectual monopoly, the critical mode can be described as intellectual competition. This competition prevails regardless of the attitude of particular individuals or schools of thought. Some of the competing ideas are tentative and invite criticism; others are dogmatic and defy opposition.

CRITICAL ATTITUDE

A critical attitude ought to be more appropriate to the circumstances of a changing world than a dogmatic one. Tentative opinions are not necessarily correct and dogmatic ones need not be completely false; but a dogmatic approach can only lose from its persuasive force when conflicting views are available: criticism is a danger, not a help. By contrast, a critical attitude can and does benefit from the criticism offered: the view held will be modified until no further valid objection can be raised. Whatever emerges from this rigorous treatment is likely to fulfill its purpose more effectively than the original proposition.

Criticism is basically unpleasant and hard to take. It will be accepted, if at all, only because it is effective. It follows that people's attitude greatly depends on how well the critical process functions; conversely, the functioning of the critical process depends on people's attitude. Thus the success of the critical process and the permanence of the critical mode of thinking are far from assured.

The great merit of the critical process is that it can provide a better understanding of reality than the traditional or, as we shall see later, the dogmatic mode. Whether it fulfills its promise depends on a number of considerations. Do people care enough about understanding reality to put up with the inconveniences of the critical process? Does reality provide a reliable criterion for evaluating competing interpretations? Is there a general agreement about the way the process is supposed to work? These questions are interconnected. We shall find that the success of the critical process varies according to the subject matter and the purpose of thinking.

SCIENTIFIC METHOD

The critical process works most effectively in natural science. Reality provides a reliable criterion for judging the truth or validity of scientific statements and there is general agreement both on the purpose of thinking and the way the critical process is supposed to function. That is because nature operates independently of what people think. Understanding the laws that govern nature is the best way to exert control over nature. Consequently, there is no conflict between seeking the truth and seeking to impose one's will on reality. At the same time, scientific knowledge serves not only to establish the truth; it also helps us in the business of living. The connection is not obvious but once it has been established it becomes irresistible. Guns are more powerful than the bow and arrow.

People might have continued to live quite happily believing that the Earth was flat, despite Galileo's experiments. What rendered his arguments irresistible was the gold and silver found in America. The practical results were not foreseen: indeed, they would not have been achieved if scientific research had been confined to purely practical objectives. Yet they provided the supreme proof for scientific method: only because there is a reality, and because man's knowledge of it is imperfect, was it possible for science to uncover certain facets of reality whose existence people had not even imagined.

Scientific method has been able to develop its own rules and conventions on which all participants are tacitly agreed. These rules recognize that no individual, however gifted and honest, is capable of perfect understanding; theories must be submitted to critical examination by the scientific community. Whatever emerges from this interpersonal process will have reached a degree of objectivity of which no individual thinker would be capable on his own. Scientists adopt a thoroughly critical attitude not because they are more rational or tolerant than ordinary human beings but because the critical process is indispensable to the success of scientific method. Their attitude is more a result of the critical process than a cause of it.

Scientific method has been very successful in the study of natural phenomena but less so in the social sphere. Nature operates independently of our wishes; society, however, can be influenced by the theories that relate to it. In natural science theories must be true to be effective; not so in the social sciences. There is a shortcut: people can be swayed by theories. The urge to abide by the conventions of science is less compelling, and the interpersonal process suffers as a result. Theories seeking to change society may take on a scientific guise in order to exploit the reputation science has gained without abiding by its conventions. The critical process offers little protection because the agreement on purpose is not as genuine as in the case of natural science. There are two criteria by which theories can be judged: truth and effectiveness—and they no longer coincide.

The remedy proposed by most champions of scientific method is to enforce the rules developed by natural science with redoubled vigor. Karl Popper has proposed the doctrine of the unity of science: the same methods and criteria apply in the study of both natural and social phenomena. I disagree. There is a fundamental difference between the two pursuits: the subject matter of the social sciences is reflexive in character and reflexivity destroys the separation between statement and fact which has made the critical process so effective in the natural sciences.

Reflexivity creates some difficulties for the critical process that are absent in the natural sciences. We need to recognize two distinctly different problems. One is that the theories can influence the subject matter to which they relate. The other is that the imperfect understanding of the participants introduces an element of uncertainty into the subject matter that renders falsifiable predictions and explanations difficult to reach.

Karl Popper was right in insisting that theories need to be falsifiable in order to qualify as scientific and he was right in pointing out that Marxism does not qualify. But he did not cast his net wide enough. He did not recognize that a basic tenet of mainstream economics, namely that financial markets tend towards equilibrium, does not qualify either. Equilibrium is an abstract concept modeled on Newtonian physics and based on assumptions that do not prevail in reality. Empirical evidence that financial markets do not exhibit a consistent tendency towards equilibrium does not, therefore, invalidate the theory.

The difficulties connected with reflexivity are not well recognized. The social sciences have tried very hard to imitate the natural sciences in order to cloak themselves in the reputation that natural science has established. Economic theory, in particular, has gone to great lengths to deny reflexivity.

By taking the conditions of supply and demand as independently given, it has managed to eliminate reflexivity from its subject matter. As a result, economic theory presents a misleading picture of reality but the distortion is difficult to demonstrate as long as social science is judged by the same criteria as natural science. Scientific theories are supposed to provide unequivocal predictions and explanations; theories that recognize reflexivity cannot possibly do so.

The critical process faces even greater difficulties outside the realm of science. The avowed aim of science is to generate knowledge; knowledge is based on true statements; the critical process is therefore firmly rooted in the pursuit of truth. Not so in other spheres of activity. The primary purpose of thinking is to advance one's personal interests, whatever they are, not to pursue truth in an abstract form unless that happens to be someone's special interest. Since people have divergent views of reality, the pursuit of truth is a very inefficient way to advance one's self-interest and few people indulge in it. Nevertheless, there is a crying need to correct misconceptions because distorted views have unintended adverse consequences. How can the need be met?

MARKET ECONOMY AND DEMOCRACY

In the economy, financial markets provide an efficient feedback mechanism for deciding whether investment decisions were correct or not. Financial markets are far from perfect. They are liable to produce initially self-reinforcing but eventually self-defeating boom-bust processes rather than equilibrium and in any case they are suited only for the allocation of scarce resources among competing private needs, not for the pursuit of common interests—those need to be decided by a political process. Nevertheless, financial markets are superior to arbitrary investment decisions. Similarly in politics a democratic form of government is more likely to avoid grievous mistakes than arbitrary rules. An authoritarian form of government must actively suppress alternative views because it can command universal acceptance only by forbidding criticism and preventing new ideas from emerging; in short, by destroying the critical mode of thinking and arresting change. If, by contrast, people are allowed to decide questions of social organization for themselves, solutions need not be final: they can be reversed by the same process by which they were reached. Everyone is at liberty to express his or her views and, if the critical process is working effectively, the view that eventually prevails may come close to representing the best interests of the participants. This is the principle of democracy.

For democracy to function properly, certain conditions must be met which may be compared to those which have made the scientific method so successful: in the first place there must be a criterion by which conflicting ideas can be judged, and in the second, there must be a general willingness to abide by that criterion. The first prerequisite is provided by the majority vote as defined by the constitution, and the second by a belief in democracy as a way of life. A variety of opinions is not enough to create democracy; if separate factions adopt opposing dogmas the result is not democracy but civil war. People must believe in democracy as an ideal: they must consider it more important that decisions be reached by constitutional means than to see their view prevail. This condition will be satisfied only if democracy does in fact produce positive results.

There is a circular relationship here: democracy can serve as an ideal only if it is effective, and it can be effective only if it is generally accepted as an ideal. This relationship has to evolve through a reflexive process in which the achievements of democracy reinforce democracy as an ideal and *vice versa*. Democracy cannot be imposed by edict.

The similarity with science is striking. The convention of objectivity and the effectiveness of scientific method are also mutually dependent on one another. Science relies on its discoveries to break the vicious circle: they speak more eloquently in its favor than any argument. Democracy, too, requires positive accomplishments: an expanding economy, intellectual and spiritual stimulation, a political system that satisfies citizen's aspirations better than rival forms of government.

Democracy is capable of such achievements. It gives free

reign to what may be regarded as the positive aspect of imperfect knowledge, namely creativity. There is no way of knowing what creativity will produce; the unforeseen results may provide the best justification for democracy just as they do for science. But progress is not assured. The positive contributions can come only from the participants. The results of their thinking cannot be predicted; they may or may not continue to make democracy a success. Belief in democracy as an ideal is a necessary but not a sufficient condition. This makes democracy as an ideal very tricky indeed. It cannot be guaranteed even by gaining universal acceptance for the ideal. Democracy simply cannot be assured, because it remains conditional on the creative energies of those who participate in it. Yet it must be regarded as an ideal if it is to prevail. Those who believe in it must put their faith in the positive aspect of imperfect knowledge and hope that it will produce the desired results.

THE QUEST FOR CERTAINTY

Democracy as an ideal leaves something to be desired. It does not provide a definite program, a clear-cut goal, except in those cases where people have been deprived of their freedom. Once people are free to pursue alternative goals, they are confronted by the necessity of deciding what their goals are. And that is where a critical attitude is less than satisfactory. It does not provide any assurance that the decisions reached are the right ones. Natural science can produce firm conclusions because it has objective criteria at its disposal. Social science is on shakier grounds because reflexivity interferes with objectivity; when it comes to deciding on political programs a critical attitude, by itself, is not much use at all. It has to be combined with a set of values and beliefs that is then subjected to a process of critical evaluation. An unwavering belief in one's self-interest may be much more powerful than a tentative search for the common interest.

The traditional mode of thinking meets the quest for certainty much more effectively than the critical mode. It draws no distinction between belief and reality: religion, or its primitive equivalent, animism, embraces the entire sphere of thought and commands unquestioning allegiance. No wonder that people hanker after the lost paradise of primeval bliss! Dogmatic ideologies promise to satisfy that craving. The trouble is that they can do so only by eliminating conflicting beliefs. This makes them as dangerous to the critical mode of thinking as the existence of alternative explanations is to the traditional mode.

OPEN SOCIETY

At the time I constructed my framework, I thought of open society as a perfectly changeable society that stands in contrast with the perfect changelessness of organic society. Since then I have changed my view. I now regard open society as a reasonably stable society that holds itself open to innovation and improvement. Sudden change and uncertainty can pose an existential threat to open society. Here I shall present the framework as I originally conceived it in the early 1960s. That was the framework that guided me when I became involved in the opening up of the Soviet system.

Subsequent revisions in the framework are recounted in Chapter 2.

Perfect Competition

A perfectly changeable society seems difficult to imagine. Surely, society must have a permanent structure, otherwise how could it support the intricate relationships of a civilization? Yet a perfectly changeable society cannot only be postulated: it has already been extensively studied in the theory of perfect competition. Perfect competition provides economic units with alternative situations that are only marginally inferior to the one which they actually occupy. Should there be the slightest change in circumstances, they are ready to move; in the meantime their dependence on present relationships is kept at a minimum. The result is a perfectly changeable society which may not be changing at all.

I regard the theory of perfect competition as unrealistic, but I shall use it as my starting point because it has been so influential. By showing how I differ from the approach taken by classical economics, I can throw more light on the concept of open society than if I tried to approach it independently. My basic objection to the theory of perfect competition is that it produces a static equilibrium, while I maintain that an open society is bound to be in dynamic disequilibrium.

Perfect competition is described by economic theory in the following way: a large number of individuals, each with their own scale of values, is faced with a large number of alternatives among which they can freely choose. If each man chooses rationally he will end up with the alternative most to his liking. Classical theory then goes on to argue that, owing to the large number of alternatives, the choice of one individual does not interfere with the alternatives available to others, so that perfect competition serves to maximize everyone's welfare.

The theory assumes that there are a large number of units, each with perfect knowledge and mobility. Each unit has its own scale of preferences and is faced with a given scale of opportunities. I consider these assumptions unrealistic. My approach is based on the lack of perfect knowledge. And perfect mobility cannot be reconciled with fixed assets and specialized skills, both of which are indispensable to the capitalistic mode of production. The reason why economists have tolerated such unacceptable assumptions for so long is that they produced results that were considered desirable in more ways than one. First, they established economics as a science comparable in status with physics. The resemblance between the static equilibrium of perfect competition and Newtonian thermodynamics is no coincidence. Second, they proved the point that perfect competition maximizes welfare.

In reality, conditions approximate those of perfect competition only when new ideas, new products, new methods, new preferences keep people and capital on the move. Mobility is not perfect: it is not without cost to move. But people are on the move nevertheless, attracted by better opportunities or dislocated by changing circumstances, and once they start moving they tend towards the more attractive opportunities. They do not have perfect knowledge but, being on the move, they are aware of a larger number of alternatives than if they occupied the same position all their lives. They will object to other people taking their places but, with so many opportunities opening up, their attachment to the existing situation is less strenuous and they will be less able to align support from others who are actually or potentially in the same situation. As people move more often, they develop a certain facility in adjusting which reduces the importance of any specialized skills they may have acquired. What we may call "effective mobility" replaces the unreal concept of perfect mobility and the critical mode of thinking takes the place of perfect knowledge. The result is not perfect competition as defined in economics but a condition I shall call "effective competition." What sets it apart from perfect competition is that values and opportunities, far from being fixed, are constantly changing.

Should equilibrium ever be reached, the conditions of effective competition would cease to apply. Units would occupy specific positions which would be less easily available to others for the simple reason that they would fight to defend them. Having developed special skills, moving would involve them in a loss. They would resist any encroachment with all their might; if necessary, they would rather take a cut in remuneration than make a move, especially as they would then have to fight someone else's vested interest. In view of their entrenched position and the sacrifices they would be willing to make to defend it, an outsider would find it difficult to compete. Instead of almost unlimited opportunities, each unit would then be more or less tied to the existing arrangement. And, not being endowed with perfect knowledge, they might not even realize the opportunities they are missing. A far cry from perfect competition!

Instability

The differences with the classical concept of perfect competition are worth pursuing. Classical economics takes both values and opportunities as independently given; I consider them reflexive. It follows that instability must be an endemic problem. This conclusion directly contradicts the classical theory of perfect competition, where the rational pursuit of self-interest is supposed to produce equilibrium. Instead of equilibrium, the free play of market forces produces a never-ending process of change in which excesses of one kind yield to those of another.

This conclusion opens a Pandora's box. Classical analysis is based entirely on self-interest; but if the pursuit of self-interest does *not* lead to a stable system, the question arises whether it is sufficient to ensure the survival of the system. The answer is a resounding "no." The stability of financial markets can be preserved only by some form of regulation. And once we make stability a policy objective, other worthy causes follow. Surely in conditions of stability, competition must also be preserved. Public policy aimed at preserving stability and competition and who knows what else is at loggerheads with the principle of *laissez-faire*. One of them must be wrong.

The nineteenth century can be invoked as an age in which *laissez-faire* was the generally accepted and actually prevailing economic order in a large part of the world. Clearly, it was not characterized by the equilibrium of economic theory. It was a period of rapid economic advance during which new methods of production were invented, new forms of economic organizations were evolving, and the frontiers of economic activity were expanding in every direction. The old framework of economic controls had broken down; progress was so rapid that there was no time for planning it; developments were so novel that there was no known method of controlling them. The mechanism of the State was quite inadequate for taking on additional tasks; it was hardly in a position to maintain law and order in the swollen cities and on the expanding frontiers.

As soon as the rate of growth slowed down, the mechanisms of state regulation began to catch up with the requirements made on it. Statistics were collected, taxes gathered, and some of the more blatant anomalies and abuses of free competition were corrected. As new countries embarked on a course of industrialization, they had the example of others before them. For the first time the state was in a position in which it could exercise effective control over industrial development and people were given a real choice between *laissez-faire* and planning. As it happened, this marked the end of the golden age of *laissez-faire:* protectionism came first and other forms of state control followed.

The principle of *laissez-faire* enjoyed a strong revival in the 1980s. President Reagan invoked the magic of the market place, and Margaret Thatcher encouraged the survival of the fittest. Since then globalization has given the owners of capital the choice to seek out the countries where they received the best treatment. This has greatly reduced the ability of individual governments to tax them and regulate them. Prevailing conditions are far removed from the unrealistic assumptions of perfect competition but they are very favorable to the untrammeled pursuit of private profit to the detriment of other considerations. Let us examine how the system works.

Freedom

Effective competition does not produce equilibrium, but it does maximize the freedom of the individual by reducing his dependence on existing relationships. Freedom is generally regarded as a right or a series of rights—freedom of speech, of movement, of worship—enforced by law or the Constitution. This is too narrow a view. I prefer to give the word a wider meaning. I regard freedom as the availability of alternatives. If the alternatives to one's current situation are greatly inferior, or if moving involves great effort and sacrifice, people remain dependent on existing arrangements and are exposed to all kinds of restraints and exploitation. If alternatives are open to them which are only marginally inferior they are free from the pressures. Should they become under pressure they merely move on. Freedom is then a function of people's ability to detach themselves from their existing positions. When the alternatives are only marginally inferior, freedom is maximized.

This is very different from how people usually look at freedom, but then freedom is generally regarded as an ideal and not as a fact. As an ideal, freedom is worth making a sacrifice for. As a fact, it consists of being able to do what one wants without having to make sacrifices for it.

People who believe in freedom as an ideal may fight for it passionately but they do not necessarily understand it. Since it serves them as an ideal, they tend to regard it as an unmitigated blessing. As a matter of fact, freedom is not devoid of undesirable aspects. When the sacrifices have borne fruit and freedom is accomplished, this may become more apparent than it was when freedom was only an ideal. The aura of heroism is dispelled, the solidarity based on a common ideal dissipated. What is left is a multitude of individuals, each pursuing their own self-interest as they perceive it. It may or may not coincide with public interest. This is freedom as it is to be found in an open society; and it may seem disappointing to those who have fought for it.

Private property

Freedom, as defined here, extends not only to human beings but to other means of production. Land and capital can also be "free" in the sense that they are not tied to particular uses but are provided with marginally graduated alternatives. This is supportive of the institution of private property.

Factors of production are always employed in conjunction with other factors, so that any change in the employment of one must have an influence on the others. As a consequence, wealth is never truly private; it impinges on the interests of others. Effective competition reduces the dependence of one factor upon another and under the unreal assumptions of perfect competition the dependence disappears altogether. This relieves the owners of productive resources of any responsibility towards other participants and provides a theoretical justification for regarding private property as a fundamental right.

It can be seen that the concept of private property needs the theory of perfect competition to justify it. In the absence of the unreal assumptions of perfect mobility and perfect knowledge, property carries with it not only rights but also obligations towards the community.

Effective competition also favors private ownership, but in a more qualified manner. The social consequences of individual decision are diffuse and adverse effects are cushioned by the ability of the affected factors to turn to alternatives. The social obligations associated with wealth are correspondingly vague and generalized, and there can be little objection to property being privately owned and managed, especially as the alternative of public ownership has worse drawbacks. But, in contrast to classical analysis, private ownership rights cannot be regarded as absolute because competition is not perfect.

Social contract

When freedom is a fact, the character of society is determined entirely by the decision of it members. Just as in an organic society the position of the members could be understood only in relation to the Whole, now the Whole is meaningless by itself and can be understood only in terms of the individuals' decisions. It is to underscore this contrast that I use the term open society. A society of this kind is likely to be open also in the more usual sense of people being able to enter and leave at will, but that is incidental to my meaning.

In a civilized society people are involved in many relationships and associations. While in organic society these are determined by tradition, in open society these are shaped by the decisions of the individuals concerned: they are regulated by written and unwritten contract. Contractual ties take the place of traditional ones.

Traditional relationships are closed in the sense that their terms and conditions are beyond the control of the interested parties. For instance, the inheritance of land is predetermined; so is the relationship between serf and landlord. Relationships are also closed in the sense that they apply only to those who are directly involved and do not concern anyone else. Contractual relationships are open in the sense that the terms are negotiated by the interested parties and they can be altered by mutual agreement. They are also open in the sense that the contracting parties can be replaced by others. Contracts are often publicly known and flagrant discrepancies between arrangements covering similar situations corrected by competition.

In a sense, the difference between traditional and contractual relationships corresponds to that between concrete and abstract thought. While a traditional relationship applies only to those who are directly involved, the terms of a contract may be considered to have universal validity.

If relationships are determined by the participants, then membership in the various institutions which constitute civilized society ought also to be the subject of a contract. It is this line of reasoning which has led to the concept of a social contract. As organically expounded by Rousseau, the concept has neither theoretical nor historical validity. To define society in terms of a contract freely entered into by completely independent individuals would be misleading; and to attribute the historical genesis of civilized society to such a contract would be an anachronism. Nevertheless Rousseau's concept pinpoints the essence of open society as clearly as Menenius Agrippa's allegory defined organic society.

Open society may be regarded as a theoretical model in which all relations are contractual in character. The existence of institutions with compulsory or limited membership does not interfere with this interpretation. Individual freedom is assured as long as there are several different institutions of roughly equal standing open to each individual so that he can choose which one to belong to. This holds true even when some of those institutions, such as the state, carry compulsory powers, and others, such as social clubs cannot ostracize them because they can contract in elsewhere.

Open society does not ensure equal opportunities to all. On the contrary, if a capitalistic mode of production is coupled with private property there are bound to be great inequalities which, left to themselves, tend to increase rather than to diminish. Open society is not necessarily classless; in fact, it is difficult—although not impossible—to imagine it as such. How can the existence of classes be reconciled with the idea of open society? The answer is simple. In an open society classes are merely generalizations about social strata. Given the high level of social mobility, there can be no class consciousness of the kind Marx spoke about. His concept applies only to a closed society, and I shall discuss it more fully under that heading.

Brave New World

Let me try to carry the concept of open society to its logical conclusion and describe what a perfectly changeable society would look like. Alternatives would be available in all aspect of existence: in personal relations, opinions and ideas, productive processes and materials, social and economic organization, and so on. In these circumstances, the individual would occupy a paramount position. Members of an organic society possess no individuality at all; in a less than perfectly changeable society, established values and relationships still circumscribe the scope of people's relation to nation, family, and their fellows and depends entirely on their own decisions. Looking at the reverse side of the coin, this means that the permanence of social relationships has disappeared; the organic structure of society has disintegrated to the point where its atoms, the individuals, float around without roots or attachments.

How the individual chooses among the alternatives is the subject matter of economics. Economic analysis therefore provides a convenient starting point; all that is necessary is to extend it. In a world in which every action is a matter of choice, economic behavior characterizes all fields of activity. That does not necessarily mean that people pay more attention to the possession of goods than to spiritual, artistic or moral values, but merely that all values can be reduced to monetary terms. This renders the principles of the market mechanism relevant to such far-ranging areas as art, politics, social life, sex and religion. Not everything that has value is subject to buying and selling because there are some values which are purely personal and therefore cannot be exchanged (e.g. maternal love); others which lose their value in the process of exchange (e.g. reputation); and yet others which it would be physically impossible or illegal to trade (e.g. the weather or political appointments); but the scope of the market mechanism would be extended to its utmost limit. Even where the operation of market forces were regulated by legislation, legislation itself would be the result of a process of haggling akin to economic behavior.

Choices arise which would not even have been imagined in an earlier age. Euthanasia, genetic engineering, brainwashing become problems of practical importance. The most complex human functions, such as thinking, may be broken down into their elements and artificially reproduced. Everything appears possible until it has been proven to be impossible.

Perhaps the most striking characteristic of a perfectly changeable society is the decline in personal relationships. What makes a relationship personal is that it is tied to a specific person. Friends, neighbors, husbands and wives would become, if not interchangeable, at least readily replaceable by only marginally inferior (or superior) substitutes; they would be subject to choice under competitive conditions. Parents and children would presumably remain fixed but the ties that connect them may become looser. Personal contact may altogether decline in importance as more efficient means of communication reduce the need for physical presence.

The picture that emerges is less than pleasing. As a mitigating factor, it should be remembered that any social system becomes absurd if it is carried to its logical conclusions, be it More's *Utopia*, Defoe's imaginary countries, Huxley's *Brave New World*, or Orwell's *1984*. Nevertheless, it should be clear by now that, as an accomplished fact, open society may prove to be far less desirable than it seems to those who live in a closed society.

The Question of Values

The great boon of open society, and the accomplishment that qualifies it to serve as an ideal, is the freedom of the individual. The most obvious attraction of freedom is a negative one: the absence of restraint. But freedom has a positive aspect, too, which is even more important. It allows people to learn to think for themselves, to decide what they want and to translate their dreams into reality. They can explore the limits of their capabilities and reach intellectual, organizational, artistic and practical achievements which otherwise they might not even suspected were attainable. That can be an intensely exciting and satisfying experience.

On the negative side, the paramount position enjoyed by individuals imposes a burden on them which may at time appear unbearable. Where can they find the values they need to make all the choices that confront them? Economic analysis takes both values and opportunities as given. We have seen that the assumption is diametrically opposed to the principle of a perfectly changeable society. It is a contradiction in terms to expect an unattached individual to operate with a fixed set of values. Values are just as much a matter of choice as everything else. The choice may be conscious and the result of much heart-searching and reflection; it is more likely to be impulsive, based on family background, advice, advertising, or some other external influence. When values are changeable, changing them is bound to become an important business activity. Individuals have to choose their sets of values under great external pressures.

If it were only a matter of consumption there would be no great difficulty. When it comes to deciding which brand of cereal to choose, the sensation of pleasure may provide adequate guidance—although even that is doubtful in light of the amount spent on advertising cereals. But a society cannot be built on the pleasure principle alone. Life includes pain, risks, dangers, and the prospect of death. If pleasure were the only standard, capital could not be accumulated, many of the associations and institutions that go to make up society could not survive, nor could many of the discoveries, artistic and technical creations that form a civilization be accomplished.

Deficiency of Purpose

When we go outside those choices that provide immediate satisfaction to the individual we find that open society suffers from what may be termed a "deficiency of purpose." By this I do not mean that no purpose can be found, but merely that it has to be sought and found by each individual for and in themselves.

Finding a purpose becomes a problem. People may try to identify themselves with a larger purpose by joining a group or devoting themselves to an ideal. But voluntary associations do not have the same reassuringly inevitable quality as organic society. One does not belong as a matter of course but as a result of conscious choice. And it is difficult to commit oneself wholeheartedly to one particular group when there are so many to choose from. Even if one does, the group is not committed in return: there is constant danger of being rejected or left out.

The same applies to ideals. Religious and social ideals have to compete with each other so that they lack that all-embracing completeness that would enable people to accept them unreservedly. Allegiance to an ideal becomes as much a matter of choice as allegiance to a group. The individual remains separate; his adherence does not signify identity but a conscious act of choice. The consciousness of this act stands between the individual and the ideal adopted.

The need to find a purpose for and in themselves places individuals in a quandary. The individual is the weakest among all the units that go to make up society and has a shorter life span than most of the institutions which depend on him. On their own, individuals provide a very uncertain foundation on which to base a system of values sufficient to sustain a structure that will outlast them and which must represent a greater value in their eyes than their own life and welfare. Yet such a value system is needed to sustain open society.

The inadequacy of the individual as a source of values may find expression in different ways. Loneliness, feelings of inferiority, guilt and futility may be directly related to a deficiency in purpose. Such psychic disturbances are exacerbated by people's tendency to hold themselves personally responsible for these feelings instead of putting their personal difficulties into a social context. Psychoanalysis is no help in this regard: whatever its therapeutic value, its excessive preoccupation with the individual tends to aggravate the problem which it seeks to cure.

The problems of the individual become greater the more wealth and power he or she possesses. Someone who can hardly make ends meet cannot afford to stop and ask about the purpose of life. But what I have called the "positive aspect of imperfect knowledge" can be relied on to make open societies affluent, so that the quandary is likely to present itself in full force. A point may be reached where even the pleasure principle is endangered: people may not be able to derive enough satisfaction from the results of their labor to justify the effort that goes into reaching them. The creation of wealth may provide its own justification as a form of creative activity; it is when it comes to the enjoyment of the fruits that signs of congestion tend to appear.

Those who are unable to find a purpose in themselves may be driven to a dogma that provides the individual with a ready-made set of values and a secure place in the universe. One way to remove the deficiency of purpose is to abandon open society. If freedom becomes an unbearable burden, closed society may appear as the salvation.

THE DOGMATIC MODE OF THINKING

We have seen that the critical mode of thinking puts the burden of deciding what is right or wrong, true or untrue, squarely on the individual. Given the individual's imperfect understanding, there are a number of vital questions—notably those that concern the individual's relation to the universe and his place in society—to which he or she cannot provide a final answer. Uncertainty is hard to bear and the human mind is likely to go to great lengths to escape from it.

There is such an escape: the dogmatic mode of thinking. It consists in establishing as paramount a body of doctrine which is believed to originate from a source other than the individual. The source may be tradition, or an ideology which succeeded in gaining supremacy in competition with other ideologies. In either case, it is declared as the supreme arbiter over conflicting views: those that conform are accepted; those that are in conflict, rejected. There is no need to weigh alternatives: every choice is already made. No question is left unanswered; the fearful specter of uncertainty is removed.

The dogmatic mode of thinking has much in common with the traditional mode. By postulating an authority which is the source of all knowledge, it attempts to retain or recreate the wonderful simplicity of a world in which the prevailing view is not subject to doubt or questioning. But it is exactly the lack of simplicity that differentiates it from the traditional mode. In the traditional mode, changelessness is a universally accepted fact; in the dogmatic mode, it is a postulate. Instead of a single universally accepted view, there are many possible interpretations but only one of them is in accord with the postulate. The others must be rejected. What makes matters complicated is that the dogmatic mode cannot admit that it is making a postulate because that would undermine the unquestionable authority that it seeks to establish. To overcome this difficulty, incredible mental contortions may be necessary. Try as it may, the dogmatic mode of thinking cannot recreate the conditions in which the traditional mode prevailed. The essential point of difference is this: a genuinely changeless world can have no history. Once there is an awareness of conflicts past and present, explanations lose their inevitable character. This means that the traditional mode of thinking is restricted to the earliest stages of man's development. Only if people could forget their earlier history would a return to the traditional mode be possible.

A direct transition from the critical to the traditional mode can thus be ruled out altogether. If a dogmatic mode of thinking prevailed for an indefinite period, history might fade out gradually—but at the present juncture this does not deserve to be regarded as a practical possibility. The choice is only between the critical and the dogmatic modes.

In effect, the dogmatic mode of thinking extends the assumption of changelessness (which permits perfect knowledge) to a world which is no longer perfectly changeless. This is no easy task. In view of man's imperfect understanding, no explanation can be fully in accord with reality. As long as observation has any bearing on what is regarded as incontrovertible truth, some discrepancies are bound to arise. The only really effective solution is to remove truth from the realm of observation and reserve it for a higher level of consciousness in which it can rule undisturbed by conflicting evidence.

The dogmatic mode of thinking therefore tends to resort to a superhuman authority such as God or History, which reveals itself to mankind in one way or another. The revelation is the only and ultimate source of truth. While men, with their imperfect intellect, argue endlessly about the applications and implications of the doctrine, the doctrine itself continues to shine in its august purity. While observation records a constant flow of changes, the rule of the superhuman power remains undisturbed. This device maintains the illusion of a well-defined permanent world order in the face of much evidence that would otherwise discredit it. The illusion is reinforced by the fact that the dogmatic mode of thinking, if successful, tends to keep social conditions unchanging. Yet even at its most successful, the dogmatic mode does not possess the simplicity that was the redeeming feature of the traditional mode.

The traditional mode of thinking dealt entirely with concrete situations. The dogmatic mode relies on a doctrine that is applicable to all conceivable conditions. Its tenets are abstractions which exist beyond, and often in spite of, direct observation. The use of abstraction brings with it all of the complications from which the traditional mode was exempt. Far from being simple, the dogmatic mode of thinking can become even more complex than the critical mode. This is hardly surprising. To maintain the assumption of changelessness in conditions that are not fully appropriate, without admitting that an assumption has been made, is a distortion of reality. One must go through complicated contortions to achieve a semblance of credibility, and pay heavy penalties in terms of mental effort and strain. Indeed, it would be difficult to believe that the human mind is capable of such self-deception if history did not provide actual examples. It appears that the mind is an instrument that can resolve any self-generated contradiction by creating new contradictions somewhere else. This tendency is given free reign in the dogmatic mode of thinking because, as we have seen, its tenets are exposed to minimum contact with observable phenomena.

With all effort devoted to resolving internal contradictions, the dogmatic mode of thinking offers little scope for improving the available body of knowledge. It cannot admit direct observation as evidence because in case of a conflict the authority of dogma would be undermined. It must confine itself to applying the doctrine. This leads to arguments about the meaning of words, especially those of the original revelation—sophistic, talmudistic, theological, ideological discussions, which tend to create new problems for every one they resolve. Since thinking has little or no contact with reality, speculation is inclined to become more convoluted and unreal the further it proceeds. How many angels can dance on the head of a needle?

What the actual contents of a doctrine are depends on historical circumstances and cannot be made the subject of generalization. Tradition may provide part of the material but, in order to do so, it must undergo a radical transformation. The dogmatic mode of thinking requires universally applicable statements, while tradition was originally couched in concrete terms. It must now be generalized in order to make it relevant to a wider range of events than it was destined for. How this can be accomplished is clearly demonstrated by the growth of languages. One of the ways in which a language adjusts itself to changing circumstances is by using in a figurative sense words that originally had only a concrete connotation. The figurative meaning retains but one characteristic aspect of the concrete case and may then be applied to other concrete cases which share that characteristic. The same method is use by preachers who take as their next text a piece of narrative from the Bible.

A doctrine may also incorporate ideas originating in an open society. Every philosophical and religious theory offering a comprehensive explanation for the problems of existence has the makings of a doctrine; all it needs is unconditional acceptance and universal enforcement. The originator of a comprehensive philosophy may not have intended to put forth a doctrine that is to be unconditionally accepted and universally enforced; but personal inclinations have little influence on the development of ideas. Once an ideology becomes the sole source of knowledge, it assumes certain characteristics which prevail irrespective of it original intention.

Since the critical mode of thinking is more powerful than the traditional mode, ideologies developed by critical thinking are more likely to serve as the basis of dogma than tradition itself. Once established, they may take on a traditional appearance. If language is flexible enough to permit the figurative use of concrete statements, it can also lend itself to the reverse process, and abstract ideas can be personified. The Old Testament God is a case in point and Frazer's *Golden Bough* offers many other examples. We may find in practice that what we call tradition incorporates many products of critical thinking translated into concrete terms.

The primary requirement of dogma is to be all-embracing. It must provide a yardstick by which every thought and action can be measured. If one could not evaluate everything in its light, one would have to cast around for other methods of distinguishing between right and wrong; such a search would destroy the dogmatic mode of thinking. Even if the validity of the dogma were not attacked directly, the mere fact that the application of the other criteria can have divergent results would tend to undermine its authority. If a doctrine is to fulfill its function as the fountain of all knowledge, its supremacy must be asserted in every field. It may not be necessary to refer to it all of the time: the land can be cultivated, pictures painted, wars fought, rockets launched—each in its own fashion. But whenever an idea or action comes into conflict with a doctrine, the doctrine must be given precedence. In this way, ever larger areas of human activity may come under its control.

The other main characteristic of dogma is its rigidity. The traditional mode of thinking is extremely flexible. As tradition is timeless, any alteration is immediately accepted not only in the present but as something that has existed since time immemorial. Not so the dogmatic mode. Its doctrines provide a yardstick by which thoughts and actions are to be judged. Hence they must be permanently fixed and no amount of transgression can justify a change. If there is a departure from the norm it must be corrected at once; the dogma itself must remain inviolate.

In the light of our inherently imperfect understanding, it is clear that new developments may clash with established doctrines or create internal contradictions in unforeseen ways. Any change represents a potential threat. To minimize the danger, the dogmatic mode of thinking tends to inhibit new departures both in thinking and in action. It does so not only by eliminating unregulated change from its own view of the universe but also by actively suppressing unregulated thoughts and actions. How far it will go in this direction depends on the extent to which it is attacked.

In contrast to the traditional mode of thinking, the dogmatic mode is inseparably linked with some form of compulsion. Compulsion is necessary to ensure the supremacy of dogma over actual and potential alternatives. Every doctrine is liable to raise questions which do not resolve themselves by mere contemplation; in the absence of an authority that defines the doctrine and defends its purity, the unity of the dogmatic view is bound to break up into conflicting interpretations. The most effective way to deal with this problem is to charge a human authority with interpreting the will of the superhuman power from which validity of doctrines can keep pace with changes occurring in reality. But no innovation other than one sanctioned by the authority can be tolerated, and the authority must have sufficient power to eliminate conflicting views.

There may be circumstances in which the authority need have little recourse to force. As long as the prevailing dogma fulfills its functions of providing an all-embracing explanation, people will tend to accept it without question. After all, the dogma enjoys monopoly: while there may be various views available on particular issues, when it comes to reality as a whole there is only one view that is acceptable. People are brought up under its aegis, they are trained to think in its terms: it is natural for them to accept it rather than to question it.

Yet when internal contradictions develop into ever more unrealistic debates, or when new events occur which do not fit in with established explanation, people may begin to question the foundations. When this happens, the dogmatic mode of thinking can be sustained only by force. The use of force is bound to have a profound influence on the evolution of ideas. Thinking no longer develops along its own lines, but becomes intricately interwoven with power politics. Particular thoughts are associated with particular interests and the victory of an interpretation depends more on the relative political strength of its proponents than on the validity of the arguments marshaled in it support. The human mind becomes a battlefield of political forces and, conversely, doctrines become weapons in the hands of warring factions.

The supremacy of a doctrine can thus be prolonged by means that have little to do with the validity of arguments. The greater the coercion employed to maintain the dogma in force, the less likely it is to satisfy the needs of the enquiring mind. When finally the hegemony of a dogma is broken, people are likely to feel that they have been liberated from terrible oppression. Wide new vistas are opened and the abundance of opportunities engenders hope, enthusiasm and tremendous intellectual activity.

It can be seen that the dogmatic mode of thinking fails to recreate any of the qualities that made the traditional mode so attractive. It turns out to be convoluted, rigid and oppressive. True, it eliminates the uncertainties that plague the critical mode but only at the cost of creating conditions which the human mind would find intolerable if it were aware of any alternatives. Just as a doctrine based on a superhuman authority may provide an avenue of escape from the shortcomings of the critical mode, the critical mode itself may appear as the salvation to those who suffer from the oppression of a dogma.

CLOSED SOCIETY

Organic society presents some very attractive features to the observer: a concrete social unity, an unquestioned belonging, an identification of each member with the collective. Members of an organic society would hardly consider this an advantage. Ignorant as they are that the relationship could be any different, only those who are aware of a conflict between the individual and the social Whole in their own society are likely to regard organic unity as a desirable goal. In other words, the attractions of organic society are best appreciated when the conditions required for its existence no longer prevail.

It is hardly surprising that throughout history mankind should have shown a yearning to return to its original state of innocence and bliss. The expulsion from the Garden of Eden is a recurrent theme. But innocence, once lost, cannot be regained—except perhaps by forgetting all experience. In any attempt to recreate artificially the conditions of organic society, it is precisely the unquestioning and unquestionable identification of all members with the society to which they belong that is the most difficult to achieve. In order to reestablish organic unity it is necessary to proclaim the supremacy of the collective. The result, however will differ from organic society in one vital respect: instead of being identical with it, individual interests become subordinated to those of the collective.

The distinction between personal and public interest raises a disturbing question as to what the public interest really is. The common interest must be defined, interpreted and, if necessary, enforced over conflicting personal interests. This task is best performed by a living ruler because he or she can adjust his or her policies to the circumstances; if it is entrusted to an institution, it is likely to be performed in a cumbersome, inflexible and ultimately ineffective manner. The institution will seek to prevent changes, but in the long run it cannot succeed.

However the common interest is defined in theory, in practice it is likely to reflect the interest of the rulers. It is they who proclaim the supremacy of the Whole and it is they who impose its will on recalcitrant individuals; unless one assumes that they are totally selfless, it is they who benefit from it. The rulers are not necessarily furthering their selfish ends as individuals but they do benefit from the existing system as a class: by definition, they are the class that rules. Since the membership of classes is clearly defined, the subordination is of one class to another. Closed society may therefore be described as a society based on class exploitation. Exploitation may occur in open society as well but, since the position of the individual is not fixed, it does not operate on a class basis. Class exploitation in Marx's sense can exist only in a closed society. Marx made a valuable contribution when he established the concept, just as Menenius Agrippa did when he compared society with an organism. Both of them, however, applied it to the wrong kind of society.

If the avowed aim of a closed society is to ensure the supremacy of one class (or race or group) over another, it may fulfill its purpose effectively. But if its aim is to bring back the idyllic conditions of an organic society, it is bound to fail. There is a gap between the ideal of social unity and the reality of class exploitation. To bridge the gap, an elaborate set of explanation is needed which is, by definition, at variance with the facts.

Getting the ideology universally accepted is the prime task of the ruling authority and the criterion of its success. The more widely an ideology is accepted, the smaller the conflict between the collective interest and the policies actually pursued, and *vice versa*. At its best, an authoritarian system can go a long way towards re-establishing the calm harmony of organic society. More often some degree of coercion needs to be employed and this fact needs to be explained away by tortuous arguments which render the ideology less convincing, requiring the use of further force until, at its worst, the system is based on compulsion and its ideology bears no resemblance to reality.

Index

PUBLICAFFAIRS is a nonfiction publishing house founded in 1997. It is a tribute to the standards, values, and flair of three persons who have served as mentors to countless reporters, writers, editors, and book people of all kinds, including me.

I. F. STONE, proprietor of *I. F. Stone's Weekly*, combined a commitment to the First Amendment with entrepreneurial zeal and reporting skill and became one of the great independent journalists in American history. At the age of eighty, Izzy published *The Trial of Socrates*, which was a national bestseller. He wrote the book after he taught himself ancient Greek.

BENJAMIN C. BRADLEE was for nearly thirty years the charismatic editorial leader of *The Washington Post*. It was Ben who gave the *Post* the range and courage to pursue such historic issues as Watergate. He supported his reporters with a tenacity that made them fearless, and it is no accident that so many became authors of influential, best-selling books.

ROBERT L. BERNSTEIN, the chief executive of Random House for more than a quarter century, guided one of the nation's premier publishing houses. Bob was personally responsible for many books of political dissent and argument that challenged tyranny around the globe. He is also the founder and was the longtime chair of Human Rights Watch, one of the most respected human rights organizations in the world.

·   ·   ·

For fifty years, the banner of Public Affairs Press was carried by its owner Morris B. Schnapper, who published Gandhi, Nasser, Toynbee, Truman, and about 1,500 other authors. In 1983 Schnapper was described by *The Washington Post* as "a redoubtable gadfly." His legacy will endure in the books to come.

Peter Osnos, *Founder and Editor-at-Large*